Anti-Aging
for
Dogs

Also by
John M. Simon, D.V.M. (with Stephanie Pederson)

What Your Dog Is Trying to Tell You
What Your Cat Is Trying to Tell You

Anti-Aging
for
Dogs

John M. Simon, D. V. M.
with
Steve Duno

PRODUCED BY THE PHILIP LIEF GROUP, INC.

St. Martin's Press New York

I dedicate this book to my wife, Joanie, my office manager, Judy, and to my entire staff, including my technicians, Bev and Kelly, my veterinary assistant, Carol, my receptionists, Laura, Jan, and Michelle, and my kennel assistant, Annie, all of whom, by doing their jobs so well, provided me with the time, energy, and peace of mind to write this book.

Library of Congress Cataloging-in-Publication Data

Simon, John, D.V.M.
Anti-aging for dogs / John Simon with Steve Duno.—1st U.S. ed.
p.   cm.
ISBN 0-312-19060-3
1. Dogs—Aging—Prevention.   2. Dogs—Longevity.   3. Dogs—Health.
4. Veterinary geriatrics.   I. Duno, Steve.   II. Title.
SF991.S554   1998
636.7'089'268—dc21   98-22879
                                                                                        CIP

First Edition: November 1998

DESIGN: JAMES SINCLAIR

10   9   8   7   6   5   4   3   2   1

Contents

General Disclaimer

This book is meant to educate and should not be used as an alternative to proper veterinary medical care. No recipes, nutritional therapy, antioxidant therapy, herbal therapy, enzyme therapy, or any other type of treatment mentioned herein should be used without qualified veterinary medical consultation and approval. In light of ongoing research and the constant flow of information, it is possible that new findings may change what we now know about these subjects.

It should be understood that since there are no formally established and conventionally accepted doses for herbal therapy, meganutrient therapy, antioxidant therapy, plant enzyme therapy, glandular therapy, and several other alternative therapies. Any such doses that are mentioned in this book are based solely on Dr. Simon's clinical experience and observations, or on those of other alternative veterinary practitioners, as opposed to controlled studies. Many of these doses far exceed the conventionally recommended doses for such nutrients, herbs, enzymes, or antioxidants. Any use of these alternative therapies should be performed only under the direct supervision of a veterinarian. No guarantee can be made that fresh raw meat will not contain parasites, dangerous bacteria, or bacterial toxins; however, Dr. Simon feels that the tremendous benefits of feeding raw meat far outweigh the minimal risks, and he routinely recommends feeding such a raw meat diet. Dr. Simon's concerns that the effects of food processing and the addition of chemicals during the manufacturing of commercial pet food may negatively impact the health of your pet are Dr. Simon's personal opinions, and the opinions of many other holistically oriented veterinarians. However, it should be understood that others will undoubtedly have different opinions. The authors and publisher disclaim responsibility for any action taken as a result of reliance on any information or advice in this book. **Your veterinarian is the best person with whom to discuss any proposed diagnostic procedures or treatment.**

Introduction

Few companions in life are as loyal, trustworthy, and caring as family dogs. The love these pets have for us is pure and unconditional; dogs are not prejudiced, and they don't hold grudges. They please and protect us, humor and amaze us with their intelligence and potential. Unfortunately, they live such short lives. As loving owners, we would dearly like to extend the lives of these favored friends, if only we could. If changing a number of conditions in our dogs' lives could effectively lengthen their time here with us, wouldn't we jump at the chance?

This book is written for owners who would like to try to implement those dietary, environmental, and lifestyle changes, and in doing so, lengthen the life of their beloved pets. Those who savor a meaningful bond with their canines, take heart; it may be possible to keep your dogs around longer than we once thought possible.

The average life span for a dog today, though a good deal longer than what it was a century ago (due to better food and health care), is still pitifully brief in comparison to our own. Living on average only ten to fifteen years, a dog rarely lives to see his twentieth birthday. After a decade or more of close, meaningful camaraderie, losing our dogs to old age is a heart-wrenching experience. Fortunately, we can take steps to help minimize illness and maximize healthy longevity in our dogs. Significant life extension for canines is now more feasible than ever before.

The marvels of modern-day science have contributed to extending the life spans of humans and pets alike. Lifesaving medical and surgical techniques, advanced detection of disease, judicious use of vaccinations against viral infections, more efficient hygienic practices, nutritional research, and other improved preventive health-care practices have all combined to create conditions favorable to ensuring longer and happier lives, while saving countless sick or injured persons and animals who would have otherwise perished. Technology as related to health, however, has been a two-edged sword; the same high-tech society responsible for such life-saving advances as magnetic resonance imaging (MRI), ultrasound technology, organ transplants, and vaccinations against killers such as polio and rabies has also given birth to a myriad of toxins that can and do rob us and our pets of health and longevity, and contribute to chronic illness such as allergies, respiratory and intestinal maladies, cancer, bacterial and viral infections, and many other unfortunate (yet avoidable) conditions.

Environmental pollution, contamination and overprocessing of the food supply, depletion of nutrients in the soil—all unfortunate by-products of the industrial society we have created—combine to reduce the effectiveness of our immune systems, as well as dramatically increase the occurrence of life-shortening conditions. The human or canine body, in effect, ages more rapidly than necessary due to the slow and steady undermining of metabolic functions by nutritional deficiencies and toxins in the environment. Toxins, combined with the increasingly hectic pace of life and the resulting increase in stress levels for humans and dogs alike, create a recipe for ill health. In the end, all of the environmental and psychological strain brought on by our high-tech society effectively cancels the many medical gains achieved over the years.

What if we could find a way to greatly enhance the nutritional status and eliminate debilitating environmental and psychological factors from our dogs' world? What effect would that have on our canine friends' life spans? What if our dogs' diets could be adjusted to eliminate harmful toxins and additives and provide maximal usable, essential nutrients? Could simple and beneficial behavioral and lifestyle changes be made to encourage safer and healthier lives, and to vitalize our dogs' immune systems, internal organs, and metabolic processes? "Yes!" is the answer proposed by this book.

The thrust of this book is to show owners how to significantly extend our dogs' life spans by initiating some relatively simple yet effective changes in diet, behavior, environment, lifestyle, and methods of treatment. By following the suggestions offered here, you enable your dog to live a happier, healthier, longer life. By counteracting metabolic poisons caused by toxic substances in the environment, establishing the correct balance of nutrients in our pets' bodies, and utilizing conventional and alternative medical techniques, we may be able to keep our four-legged friends with us for a much longer and happier time.

PART I

Understanding the Process

What Is Aging?

Aging can best be defined as a natural progression and irreversible impairment of bodily functions that result in a reduction of an organism's ability to adapt to both internal and external stress. As an animal ages, she becomes progressively more vulnerable to disease and injury due, in part, to an increased inability to renew or repair tissues throughout her body. As a dog ages, her organs lose their functional reserves and regenerative powers, and so they begin to function less efficiently. Because an older animal has less reserve strength, her recovery from illness is markedly slower. The animal in question gradually experiences a reduced capacity to cope with environmental concerns such as walking, running, finding food, and self-defense. She gradually experiences a progressively decreasing mental capacity; memory often suffers, as does overall neuromuscular response. Degenerative changes occur in the organs and tissues; the various systems of the body begin to suffer increasing losses in performance. The lungs do not process oxygen as well, the liver cannot detoxify metabolic waste as efficiently, and the heart does not pump blood as powerfully.

Are all of these symptoms of aging inevitable or might they be delayed, or perhaps avoided, indefinitely? Are all animals, humans and dogs included, unavoidably programmed to slowly wind down like the mainspring of a pocket watch, eventually losing the race of time? Or, could much of aging be a disease from which we all suffer, one that awaits a treatment or cure, as did malaria, scurvy, glaucoma, and whooping cough?

Most of us have experienced the delight of a frisky young puppy around the home, cavorting, playing, and getting into all sorts of mischief as she grows and learns about her world. The strength and vigor of such a young companion is captivating and motivating to us all, making us all feel young. Puppies help us enjoy life to the fullest, adding a healthy, exuberant perspective to everyday tasks.

As that puppy grows into adulthood, she takes on the appearance and size of her parents, and in varying degrees reflects their temperaments and personalities. During her physical prime, the dog enjoys countless hours of play and a wide spectrum of activities. The combination of an active, athletic body and sharp, curious mind makes our best friend one of the most endearing characters imaginable. Few can resist a happy dog's charms, and fewer still wish to see their beloved pet lose even an iota of vitality or mental sharpness.

Unfortunately, most dogs do begin to slow down significantly by the time they reach 7 or 8 years of age. The first signs most of us notice are a gradual increase in weight and a slight graying of the coat, particularly around the face. A slow, almost imperceptible clouding of the lenses of the eyes often begins at this time, a result of protein buildup and its resulting thickening of each lens. That 7- to 8-year-old dog, although beginning to show the first signs of aging, nevertheless remains quite active and alert, participating in nearly all her favorite activities without interruption.

As she continues to age, her metabolism begins to slow, which contributes to a gain in weight and a decrease in activity. The dog may begin sleeping more, and could begin experiencing gradual losses of hearing and vision. Also, joint problems, such as arthritis, may appear, making running and jumping more difficult or even painful. A once-athletic pet, capable of leaping a five-foot fence, may now have to take the long way around. Sprains, muscle pulls, ligament tears, and other injuries become more likely as the dog approaches the decade mark. Dental problems surface, including cavities, lost or broken teeth, and periodontal disease. Lungs, once able to process oxygen at an amazing rate, begin to suffer reduced efficiency, resulting in less stamina and quicker exhaustion during exercise and play.

As the dog continues to age, other signs become prominent. The digestive process may begin to lose its efficiency, resulting in bouts of constipation, diarrhea, indigestion, or vomiting. All internal organs, including the heart, begin to operate on a diminished level, making overall functions less effective. Your once-frisky companion begins to feel the effects of age creeping up. As an owner, you must learn to come to terms with that.

Humans, living an average of seventy to eighty years, tend to show signs of age very gradually; we often don't notice our family members or friends getting older unless we are separated from them for an extended time. Dogs, who have a more abbreviated life span of ten to fifteen years, show signs of aging proportionally much later in life, and go downhill much more quickly. This may catch owners by surprise, leaving them little time to deal with the situation.

Anti-Aging Defined

This book's definition of anti-aging, or life extension, is quite broad, referring to any approach that enhances both the quality and length of life of our canine friends. More than just long lives, we want good health; perhaps the term "health span" is more appropriate here than "life span." Our goal is to help our canine friends enjoy more time in their healthy and happy middle age, rather than in sickly, uncomfortable old age.

One way of looking at changing life spans is to compare the meaning of *mean life span* to *maximum life span*. Mean life span refers to the average life span of a certain breed of dog, whereas maximum life span refers to the maximum age limit of an individual dog within that breed.

Causes of Aging

Understanding what the aging process is, what causes it, and how it works helps us establish strategies for the "war against aging." Basically, an aging animal gradually loses the ability to replace old or damaged cells with new ones. This deficit eventually wipes out functional organ reserve, and results in the appearance of chronic diseases that are commonly associated with aging, such as arthritis, senility, or loss of sensory capabilities.

The aging process can be divided into two basic types. *Genetic aging* refers to the animal's genetically programmed life span. Although genetic aging is not thoroughly understood, one theory maintains that cells have a limited number of times that they can replicate; another theory is that the brain reaches a point when it shuts off certain vital functions. Because this area of knowledge is limited, this book focuses on preventing, or reducing, the other type of aging: *random aging*. However, the book draws attention to what type of aging is genetically programmed or predetermined by the dog's breed.

Random aging has numerous causes, from sources both inside and outside the body. Sources include toxins in the air, soil, water, and food; damage from ultraviolet light and depletion of the ozone layer; nutritional deficiencies; free-radical damage; physical trauma; psychological stress; and bacterial, viral, and parasitic infections. The effects from any or all of these sources accumulate through an animal's lifetime, taking their toll on her immune system, antioxidant defense system, and detoxification system. The accumulated failures of these protective mechanisms result in cellular death, tissue destruction, and organ damage. Cumulated damage to vital organs reduces the organs' functional reserves. When these reserves are exhausted, clinical disease, with its many symptoms, becomes obvious.

A slowing of the biochemical response to toxins and diminished organ reserve function are consistent characteristics of aging. Although damage to one organ may be more apparent, illness in older dogs is rarely limited to just one disease. In all likelihood, aging organs are at various stages of dysfunction. Thus, aging and disease create a circular, snowball effect: Aging increases the body's susceptibility to disease, while disease increases the rate of random damage that leads to aging. For this reason, we must do all we can to limit any unnecessary damage to the body's systems, while building up its reserves. Nevertheless, we also must acknowledge that the results will ultimately be limited by the programmed aging tendencies that are dictated by our pets' genetic heritage.

Four Theories of Aging

A number of theories exist to explain the hows and whys of aging. Interestingly, findings from numerous studies show that the biochemistry of aging is similar among all animals. Therefore, much of the information gained through research on humans can be, and has been, applied to dogs (although making note of the metabolic differences is necessary).

Ultimately, the cause(s) of aging may be explained by a combination of theories, just as aging is a result of a number of degenerative process. Following are four of the most common theories used in designing approaches to slowing the aging process.

THE GENETIC THEORY

This theory postulates that, after a preset period of time, the body's cells are genetically programmed to end their innate repair-and-maintenance functions. In short, aging is coded into our (and our pets') DNA, and is additionally impacted by toxins in our environment such as radiation or viruses. Diagnostic tests are now available to detect accelerated DNA damage in humans. By providing the cells with the basic building blocks of DNA (through diet and herbal, vitamin, and mineral supplementation), this type of damage is more easily repaired.

THE WEAR-AND-TEAR THEORY

This theory blames aging on cell and organ damage that results from overuse and abuse. One approach to handling this situation is to stimulate the immune system's innate ability to prevent disease and repair damage.

THE NEUROENDOCRINE THEORY

According to this theory, aging is caused by a reduction of those hormones that are responsible for helping the body regulate certain critical functions. Dietary supplementation of these hormones attempts to slow the aging process by returning hormonal regulatory control to the body.

THE FREE-RADICAL THEORY

The term *oxidation* refers to what happens to metals, foods, animals, and plants when exposed to oxygen for extended periods of time. Metals rust. Foods tend to spoil, their fats becoming rancid. Living tissue that is exposed to prolonged periods of oxidation ages prematurely and develops disease. Oxidation in our dogs' bodies occurs as a result of the formation and presence of *free radicals*, extremely reactive and highly unstable charged atoms and molecules that attempts to combine with the normal atoms and molecules of the cells. In the process, these free radicals damage the cell's membrane as well as its DNA, causing major health problems in the animal.

In a healthy dog, free radicals are routinely neutralized by the body's antioxidant defense system, which consists of specific enzymes, vitamins, minerals, and amino acids that combine with the free radicals, neutralizing them and preventing cellular damage. Your dog's antioxidant system consists of antioxidant enzymes synthesized in the body, and antioxidant nutrients (such as vitaimins and minerals) taken into the body. The antioxidant enzymes are the most potent, and consist primarily of *superoxide dismutase (SOD)*, *catalase, glutathione peroxidase, and coenzyme Q10.* The antioxidant nutrients consist of:

- Vitamins A, B-complex, C, and E
- Beta-carotene and bioflavonoids
- The minerals selenium, zinc, copper, magnesium, manganese, and iron

Next to a fresh, nutritious diet, pure water, an unpolluted environment free from stress, and an abundance of love and companionship, providing your pet with antioxidants may be the most effective way to slow down the aging process. Besides retarding the aging process and preventing disease, antioxidants can also be used to treat degenerative organ diseases such as congestive heart failure, chronic kidney disease, allergies, immune deficiency disease, auto-immune disease, and arthritis. Antioxidants treat disease conditions directly by combining with and neutralizing toxic free radicals before they have chance to injure or kill cells. By putting a halt to this cascading process, organ failure and disease is prevented.

If a dog's antioxidant defense system becomes stressed (a condition often resulting from an overload of bacteria, viruses, chemical food additives, pesticides, deficient diets, allergies, prolonged drug use, stress, cancer, ultraviolet light, and pollution), the number of free radicals in her body goes up tremendously, eventually exceeding the ability of her antioxidant defense system to neutralize them. Whem this occurs, free radicals create physiological havoc, destroying tissue all over the dog's body. This process is at the root of the processes we refer to as aging and disease.

By supplementing your dog's diet with antioxidants, you can replenish and strengthen her antioxidant defense system. This will aid in stemming the tide of disease, and help delay the aging process. In addition, antioxidants function as anti-inflammatories and immune stimulants, further helping to stem the onset of illness, disease, and aging.

Cellular Regeneration

Your dog's body is constantly generating new cells to replace the ones that die. A natural process, this repair-and-replace function remains fairly constant throughout your dog's life. When the number of damaged or dying cells begin to outnumber the quantity of replacement cells and the efficacy of repair, the dog begins to slow down and, in our eyes, age. A dog suffering from excessive tissue damage, combined with inadequate repair, ages faster than one who is able to repair and replace cells at the preferred rate.

Your dog may suffer degenerative damage to his various internal tissues in many ways, some more obvious than others. These include injury, illness and infection, improper diet, toxins, allergies, stress, free-radical buildup, malfunctioning inflammatory system, inadequate rest, and overactivity. The basics of preventing excess cell damage and encouraging the regenerative process involve minimizing damaging conditions and avoiding harmful substances, while supporting any and all conditions that might help cell repair. By preventing the buildup of damaged and dying cells, you can help extend your dog's life span—and quality of life. Ways to avoid cellular damage and improve cellular regeneration include:

- Make your dog's environment as safe as possible by avoiding potentially harmful situations.
- See the vet at least once a year to detect, prevent, or treat illnesses that could accelerate cell degeneration.
- Ensure that your dog receives all essential nutrients to support her ability to repair and replace damaged and dying cells.
- Ensure that the formation and accumulation of damaging free radicals is kept to a bare minimum.
- Remove as many toxins as possible from your dog's environment and food.
- Identify and remove any allergic substances from the dog's diet and environment.

- Reduce stress in your dog's world to create less fatigued immune, regulatory, and inflammatory systems.
- Provide your dog with good hygiene, grooming, and dental care to reduce the stress placed on the immune system by bacteria.
- Ensure that your dog gets enough sleep and rest, which provides the time for regeneration to occur.
- Exercise your dog to promote strong bone and muscle development; improve digestive, cardiovascular, and respiratory functions; lower blood pressure; avoid obesity; and generally enhance metabolism—all of which contribute to a more efficient repair-and-replacement process.

The Relationship Between Disease and Aging

Everyone accepts that aging is accompanied by illness. However, we often overlook that the reverse is also true: Illness may permanently damage tissues, which depletes the organs' functional reserves and accelerates aging. Whether occurring as a single episode or as a chronic condition, disease brings increased free-radical production that damages cells. This cellular damage, in turn, brings further free-radical production. The body's antioxidant defense system comes to the rescue and neutralizes the free radicals—as long as its reserves hold out. Meanwhile, the immune, detoxification, and inflammatory systems attempt to repair the damage that has already occurred. If the dog's body is overstressed—whether emotionally or due to toxins, physical trauma, allergens, or pathogens—the body's systems become exhausted, functional organ reserves become depleted, symptoms of disease appear, organ failure occurs, and aging is accelerated. This book focuses on how preventing disease prolongs life.

One definition for health is simply the absence of disease. *Clinical disease* is present when a dog develops outward, visible symptoms and laboratory tests indicate an abnormality. If a dog experiences damage to a tissue or organ but continues acting "healthy" and shows no abnormal findings on routine laboratory tests, she suffers from *subclinical disease*. This apparently healthy animal is not truly healthy, making us question what health really means.

The absence of clinical symptoms is no guarantee of good health, a view that departs from the way medicine has been practiced for the past century. Most of our dogs' organs, when functioning at their best, have a reserve capacity of roughly six times what is necessary for normal, symptom-free function. As our dogs encounter the stresses of life, both internally and externally, they all drain a little more from their functional organ reserves. As these reserves diminish, symptoms may not be noticeable, yet our pets have dropped to a lower level on the health scale (which places optimum wellness, or full functional organ reserves, at the top and death at the bottom). This decrease of reserves brings further susceptibility to organ dysfunction, creating a state of health that is less than optimal.

If we want to prevent illness and maintain a state of superb health for our dogs, we must first learn to recognize their bodies' imbalances and correct them. As such, the prevention of illness is synonymous with maintaining strong immune, detoxification, and antioxidant defense systems, which ultimately result in extending life by maximizing functional organ reserves. *Primary prevention,* quite different from what has been conventionally called preventive medicine, includes avoiding environmental and dietary toxins, feeding a highly digestible, toxin-free, nutritionally balanced and complete diet, changing overly stressful lifestyles, and providing regular veterinary nutritional and lifestyle consultation. *Secondary prevention* includes early diagnosis of disease through routine health exams or lab tests.

The four major factors related to the causes of aging are also relevant to disease: genetics, environment, nutrition, and lifestyle. Though genetics sets the ultimate limit on our ability to affect our pets' aging and susceptibility to diseases, the latter three of these factors all involve certain levels of stress that are put on our pets' systems. Bear in mind that stress is not always a negative experience. Positive stress occurs when our dogs enjoy the challenge of playing Frisbee or catch for an hour—and would choose to continue endlessly if we had the inclination. Negative stress, involuntarily imposed on our dogs, weakens, rather than strengthens, them. We face the challenge of creating the most positive environment, both inside and out, for our best friends. Our goal is to make this challenge an uplifting and rewarding experience for both us and our dogs—for many years to come.

Medicine's Role in
Life Extension

Medicine can be defined as the art and science of the prevention and treatment of illness and disease. Once early cultures began domesticating sheep, goats, cattle, horses, chickens, and pigs, people began using medical practices to keep animals, as well as themselves, healthy. Because early humans based their beliefs about illness on supernatural causes, such as evil spirits or vengeful gods, treatment for most maladies consisted of the incantation of magic spells, charms, and complex rituals often lasting hours or even days. Though largely ineffective in affecting the course of illnesses, these early practitioners did begin to utilize herbs, roots, seeds, leaves, and mineral substances, eventually incorporating them into effective treatments for numerous conditions, including diarrhea, headaches, fever, skin rashes, fractures, and even tumorous growths.

The increasing diversity of dog breeds over the centuries was driven by the need to have dogs perform a myriad of tasks. Early breeders, through trial and error, learned much about inherited traits and how to adapt an animal's structure and temperament to best suit a specific task. Medicine, however, did not make great strides until the nineteenth and twentieth centuries, when the world saw an explosion of knowledge in all fields. Since then, a deeper understanding of the workings of human and animal physiology has developed, even down to the molecular level. The mechanics of infection are understood; vaccines for killer diseases, such as polio, rabies, distemper, and tetanus, were discovered and administered to millions;

clinical research techniques have improved; and university medical schools have required courses that are standardized worldwide.

Veterinary medicine has benefited tremendously from these advances, as a burgeoning human population requires many more healthy, prolific farm animals than every before, giving the occupation of veterinarian a new importance. "Companion" pets also are popular; millions of cats and dogs are now "part of the family" and need medical attention just as much as other family members.

Conventional Medicine

Over the past twenty-five years, advancements in the understanding and treatment of cancers and complex infectious diseases have been innumerable. These advancements have been accompanied by an increasing awareness of the role that the immune system plays in preventing illness. Scientific advances have led to improved medical technologies that make diagnosis and treatment much easier for both humans and animals. In addition, ongoing research into genetics and psychogenic (mentally derived) disorders has opened new pathways for the prevention of illnesses that were once considered untreatable.

Conventional medicine uses time-honored tests and methods, including a thorough physical exam, blood, urine, and fecal testing, X rays, blood chemistry screens, cytology, electromylograms, electroretinograms, needle-guided biopsies, ultrasounds, CAT scans and MRIs, electrocardiograms, endoscopic examinations, allergy testing, and judicious vaccination. To diagnose and treat disease, other conventional therapeutic procedures include surgery, immunizations, anesthesia, drug and intravenous fluid therapies, reconstructive techniques, advanced dental procedures, laser surgery, organ transplants, cataract surgery, endoscopic joint surgery, artificial insemination, heart-valve replacement, hemodialysis for kidney disease, and physical therapy.

The conventional approach to medicine, traditionally one of diagnosis and treatment of existing conditions, has certainly produced outstanding, lifesaving results over many years. As most persons or pets do not see a physician until an illness is clearly present, this approach is often effective in treating symptoms and bringing the patient back to normal health: conventionally defined as the lack of any symptoms. Physicians who practice a purely conventional approach to medicine act the part of a detective, first searching for clues to identify the offending culprit, determining what damage has been done, then deciding on a course of action to rid the human or animal patient of the invasive malady.

Conventional medicine's major role is to monitor, control, and alleviate symptoms and conditions, and not to aid the patient's body in an attempt to heal itself or avoid getting sick in the first place. Too often, conventional healing techniques merely mask a more chronic, underlying condition, namely one or more elemental insufficiencies in the patient's body. For example, a 7-year-old, chronically obese golden retriever, suffering from diabetes, is treated by a veterinarian with insulin to help her body regulate amounts of blood sugar. Though this course of action is proper, the condition itself may have been avoided entirely if the owner had provided a high-quality, meat-based, allergen- and toxin-free diet—and had regulated the dog's calories and provided more exercise early on. There is a high probability that this diabetic condition could have been avoided entirely if a veterinarian had put the dog on a preventive health regimen five years earlier, before any diabetic symptoms appeared.

Conventional medicine deals very well with acute conditions that often require immediate and often lifesaving treatments, such as surgery to remove an intestinal blockage or malignant growth, the administration of intravenous fluids to help save a severely dehydrated pet from certain death, or the proper use of cortisone or powerful antibiotic medications to save a dog from shock or a lethal infection such as pneumonia. Time-honored veterinary practices such as the setting of a broken leg or the judicious use of vaccines in puppies to help prevent life-threatening diseases such as rabies, parvovirus, and distemper are also supported and encouraged.

Conventional medicine's major disadvantage is that it encourages owners to expect quick and easy solutions for what are often complex, long-standing problems, through the use of a "quick-fix" drug or surgical technique. Modern drugs are often lifesavers, but they also can create a false sense of security by cloaking deeper problems. Injections of cortisone, for example, can quickly relieve scratching, musculoskeletal pain, and autoimmune disease, yet do not address the root cause of these problems. Without an exploration of causation, the affected animal continues to receive injections that suppress symptoms and the immune system, but do not eliminate the cause of the problem. Often the suppression of symptoms drives the disease even deeper, eventually resulting in a complete failure of the affected organ or organ system. Symptoms, for the most part, should be considered the expression of a process wherein the immune system is attempting to heal itself by removing or neutralizing toxins. When symptoms are suppressed, the body still must fight the toxins and their effects—yet to the pet owner, the disease may appear momentarily cured.

In addition, reliance on drug-dependent methodologies can create other problems, particularly undesirable physical and psychological side effects. Diarrhea, constipation, allergic reactions, lethargy, aggression, insomnia, panting, increased thirst, weakness, elevated blood pressure, and even seizures can result from administering certain drugs to canines. Often these side effects are as bad or worse than the original condition they were prescribed to alleviate. For instance, some dogs can develop diarrhea after being prescribed a certain type of antibiotic for a skin infection, due to the antibiotics effectively killing off the "good" bacteria essential for normal bowel function.

Alternative Medicine

Though reliance on conventional drug-based methodologies remains strong, particularly in the United States, the past decade has seen a rise in popularity of alternative forms of medicine, both for humans and animals. Many consumers and physicians alike feel that the conventional approach leaves much to be desired and that reasonable alternative or "complementary" therapies should be explored. Geared more toward maintenance of health and prevention of illness, alternative practitioners take a more *holistic* approach by considering the entire body (as opposed to just the diseased part) and the physiological and psychological forces acting on it. Symptoms are considered an expression of the body's instinctive attempt to expel the toxins causing an illness.

Holistic medicine recognizes the roles of diet, lifestyle, and environment, as well as the patient's emotional state, in maintaining good, strong health. An unhappy, nervous German shepherd may become physically ill even when no outside physical agents have acted upon him. Emotional stress can cause illnesses ranging from rashes to dehydration and even severe gastrointestinal disorders, simply by overtaxing a dog's already strained or genetically weak immune system. Pushed too far, the dog's natural bodily defense mechanisms can no longer keep up, and he becomes ill. Holistic medicine attempts to address both the emotional and physical, seeking a balance between the patient and his environment. The use of synthesized drugs is avoided unless absolutely necessary; instead more natural remedies are chosen whenever possible (e.g., herbs, vitamins, and other supplements).

Following are some of the more important guiding principles that are common to most holistic canine therapies:

1. The pet's body is capable of healing itself if given the proper es
   sentials for health, including proper nutrients, a healthy envi-

ronment free of toxins, and a lifestyle that supports the body's innate healing mechanism.

2. Holistic medicine treats the pet's body as a whole, not as a collection of independent parts. It treats a functional imbalance rather than a group of symptoms.

3. Holistic medicine sees symptoms as an expression of the immune system's attempt to heal the body. Therefore, symptoms should not be suppressed and the immune system should be supported.

4. The veterinarian or physician treats his patients' illness by utilizing an approach that balances the immune system and helps to detoxify the body. The veterinarian does not directly heal the body—he provides support for the immune system.

5. Proper nutrition is the bedrock of good health and well-being.

6. Pet owners must play an active role in their pets' health care, rather than relinquishing responsibility to their vet. Good communication between doctor and client is very important.

7. The psychological state of the dog and owner has a great effect on the pet's overall health.

Alternative Therapies

Therapies that honor a more holistic approach to medicine include acupuncture, chiropractic, massage therapy, herbal therapy, homeopathy, bach flower therapy, and detoxification therapy and fasting, which are all addressed in the following sections.

ORTHOMOLECULAR NUTRITIONAL MEDICINE AND MEGANUTRIENT THERAPY

Orthomolecular nutritional medicine is a branch of nutritional therapy that attempts to promote good health and treat disease (in humans and canines) by varying concentrations of essential substances in the body. Its practitioners believe that raising the levels of certain nutrients beyond arbitrarily established minimum daily requirements is an essential key to achieving optimal health. First introduced by Dr. Linus Pauling, orthomolecular medicine utilizes megadoses of vitamins and minerals to prevent disease and promote good health. The regular use of nutritional supplements such as digestive enzymes, fatty and amino acids, antioxidants, probiotics, natural hormones, and herbal bitters are also part of the orthomolecular regimen. In addition, the reduction of simple sugars, heavy metals (such as lead, mercury, and arsenic), artificial chemical additives, and other environmental toxins is strongly supported by practitioners of this branch of therapy.

ACUPUNCTURE

This ancient Chinese healing practice is based on the idea that redirecting fundamental energy flow in the body can promote better health. It is designed to stimulate certain "acupoints" on the patient's body, through the use of thin sterile needles accurately positioned by a trained veterinary acupuncturist. Many Western physicians now admit that acupuncture does seemingly work to reduce neuromuscular pain. What is not as readily acknowledged is that it is also very effective in balancing the immune system and in treating internal organ diseases such as kidney, liver, and heart disease as well as intestinal problems including diarrhea, constipation, megacolon, and megaesophagus. Dogs with fecal and urinary incontinence also respond well to this approach. Acupuncture therapy has proven particularly effective for treating pain associated with hip, back, pelvic, and knee disorders. The acupuncturist traditionally uses needles, but also may choose finger pressure, electrical stimulation, heat, lasers, and vitamin B_{12} injections. The International Veterinary Acupuncture Society (IVAS) can supply you with a list of certified veterinary acupuncturists.

CHIROPRACTIC

For thousands of years, physical manipulation of the body has brought patients back to optimal health. Chiropractic, a drugless therapy, has helped millions worldwide and is increasingly included in veterinarians' repertoire for treating dogs, cats, horses, and other domestic animals with various illnesses—particularly neck, back, hip, and shoulder problems. The basic theory of chiropractic states that misaligned skeletal body structures interfere with a host of processes in the body, particularly the circulation of blood and flow of nerve impulses down the spinal cord and out into the many branching nerves of the body. These affected nerves causes disorders in all areas of the body that are supplied by nerves (including internal organs). When the offending body part (most often the vertebral column) is realigned, the body is supported in returning to a normal state.

Dogs, being active, athletic creature, often injure themselves while jumping or cavorting in play. These pets can benefit from chiropractic, a healthier alternative to drugs that may only mask a problem temporarily. Skilled veterinary chiropractors undergo long hours of chiropractic study in addition to their traditional veterinary schooling. The American Veterinary Chiropractic Association (AVCA) or your veterinarian can supply you with a list of local veterinarians who are qualified to treat your pet through chiropractic.

MASSAGE THERAPY

Massage therapy has become popular as a treatment for dogs undergoing physical or psychological stress. In addition to relieving muscle tension and pain, massage can increase blood flow, accelerate the metabolization of toxic products in the muscles, encourage healing of injured tissues, and even significantly reduce stress. Persons and animals undergoing massage therapy tend to become calmer and more relaxed, which, in turn, leads to lower blood pressure. Hyperactive or nervous dogs who undergo a regular program of massage therapy learn to calm down significantly, which allows them to concentrate better. Professional dog trainers and canine behaviorists have long known this, and often incorporate massage into their training sessions. Shiatsu massage, a technique that blends the benefits of both massage and acupuncture, can provide the patient with lasting relief from pain and dysfunction.

HERBAL THERAPY

Herbal therapy emphasizes the application of unique herbs, leaves, stems, roots, flowers, and other plant-based materials to stimulate healing and good health. Herbs have been used for many centuries by Eastern and Western cultures alike, and their power as natural "pharmaceuticals" cannot be disputed.

Herbs are composed of many ingredients known as *phytochemicals,* which have the potential to promote both healing and good health in general. Many pharmaceutical drugs used by conventional medicine today were originally discovered and extracted from plants: for example, digitalis, atropine, and morphine. Herbs differ from plant-derived drugs in the following way: Whereas a drug is a single, isolated, extracted, or synthesized chemical structure, herbs contain sometimes hundreds of ingredients that work together to produce a total effect. By isolating and supplying only the so-called active ingredient, drug companies have sacrificed all the other balancing and supporting ingredients. Consequently, drugs are much more likely to produce dangerous side effects than are their herbal counterparts.

Herbal remedies have achieved excellent results over the years in the treatment of animals. Disorders ranging from skin rashes to bladder infections, constipation or diarrhea, and even heart, kidney, and liver disease have been successfully treated using a variety of herbal applications. Herbal therapies work well when used in conjunction with other holistic therapies, such as acupuncture and chiropractic.

HOMEOPATHY

Homeopathy's primary premise is that a substance given at full strength, which produces symptoms similar to the disease being treated, will cure that disease when the substance is administered in an extremely dilute form. The homeopath closely examines the patient's personal medical history to obtain an overall health and behavioral profile, then matches this profile with a "remedy." Over two thousand of these remedies, carefully catalogued over the years, are successfully used to treat physical and behavioral maladies in dogs ranging from arthritis and indigestion to allergies and anxiety.

BACH FLOWER THERAPY

Similar but not identical to homeopathic remedies, these flower distillations are used to treat emotional imbalances in the patient on the premise that if you heal the mind you heal the body. Bach flower remedies have been used by veterinarians to help dogs overcome fear and anxiety, which in turn helps the dog's physiology return to normal.

DETOXIFICATION THERAPY AND FASTING

An important approach to healing currently used by alternative practitioners around the world involves reducing the buildup of harmful toxins in the body through fasting and increased water intake, and through nutritional therapies that promote increased liver, kidney, and intestinal function, as well as provide support to the antioxidant defense system. By ridding the body of these toxins, the immune and inflammatory systems become healthier and stronger and disease and the aging process is slowed.

A Functional Compromise

Both conventional and alternative branches of medicine offer helpful and often lifesaving therapies for your dog. Rather than take an adversarial point of view, this book chooses to utilize both branches of treatment in a complementary fashion to arrive at an effective course of action, one best suited to heal and to maintain and increase the good health of our dogs. This book strongly supports whatever works, be it conventional or alternative, to promote life extension and improve everyday health. It pursues prevention as a path to life extension and, to that end, embraces holistic approaches for their ability to avoid illness and injury, increase immune-system response, and create the healthiest conditions possible for your dog.

Aging's Effects on
Your Dog's Systems

As a dog ages, all of her individual body systems begin to show gradual decreases in function. A 2-year-old boxer's digestive system, for instance, processes food faster and more efficiently than a 12-year-old of the same breed. The older dog has a decreased respiratory capacity and immune response, a slower recovery from injury, and a reduced muscle mass. As in humans, each system's slow decline in function, when cumulatively considered, contributes to the general "winding down" process. This chapter focuses on how aging affects the particular body systems, describing specifically how and why the function of each is affected by the passing of years. This progressive degeneration of the body's systems leads to aging and eventual death.

As owners, we must realize that anything we can do to slow this process down will result in longer lives for our loving pets. We also must realize that premature degeneration of the various body systems, if caught early, is often reversible by altering the diet and environment of the dog in question. A dog who eats a nutritionally deficient diet suffers a more rapid degeneration than one eating a diet rich in vitamins, minerals, enzymes, fatty acids, fiber, antioxidants, and other substances vital to maintain proper function of the organ systems. A dog living in a polluted, toxic environment certainly suffers from the effects of these poisons as well as the free radicals they generate, and as a result, has accelerated degeneration of her body's systems. By clearly understanding how the degeneration of the various organ systems occur, you are better prepared to combat the process, slowing it down enough to keep your dog around longer than once thought possible.

Proper lifestyle and nutrition habits can profoundly affect the processes described for each of the following body systems. Suggestions for changing these habits and improving on other contributing conditions are discussed in detail later in the book.

The Metabolic Effects of Aging

A dog's metabolism begins to slow down significantly by the sixth or seventh year of life, and continues to do so as the dog ages. Reaction time for muscles and nerves slows down, as does the animal's overall level of activity. This slowdown decreases the dog's caloric requirements by 20 to 40 percent during the last one-third of her life. The ability for cells to regenerate also decreases. As a result, injuries take longer to heal. The slowdown also causes a slight decrease in body temperature, which can reduce the effectiveness of key enzymes in the body, and create a more hospitable environment for certain bacteria and viruses.

The older dog also has a harder time keeping warm, and may not be able to tolerate extremes of temperature and climate as well as she once did. She does not metabolize food, drugs, or supplements as quickly as a younger animal. The older dog also has a decreased sensitivity to thirst, leading to dehydration, premature aging of the skin, poor digestion, and a host of other problems.

Due to the decrease in the metabolic rate, the older dog's muscle mass is reduced at the same time that her percentage of body fat increases. Less muscle and more fat generally mean an increased strain on the cardiovascular system, which is already affected by age in its own right.

Oxidation (the process by which free radicals are formed) increases with age, as the production of antioxidant enzymes (particularly in the liver) decreases. A decline in hormonal secretions also leads to a reduction in many bodily functions, including overall metabolism, which contributes to an increased rate of tissue degeneration.

The Cardiovascular System

The dog's cardiovascular system consists of the heart and the veins and arteries, which are the branching system of vessels that carry blood to and from all areas of the body. Essential to the survival of all cells, the blood pumped by the heart carries oxygen, nutrients, and other important chemicals to all tissues, enabling them to thrive and function. Without a properly functioning cardiovascular system, a dog would surely suffer premature aging and death.

Though dogs do not generally suffer from cardiovascular disease as frequently as humans, degenerative problems do occur with increasing regularity among dogs over nine years of age. As your dog grows older, the overall weight of her heart increases while its overall pumping efficiency decreases. Degenerative lesions of the heart valves can appear, contributing to decreased cardiac output to the whole body as well as a reduced flow of nutrients and oxygen to the heart muscle itself. The walls of the larger arteries in the dog's body can become thicker and less flexible, affecting circulation to the brain and to the extremities. Maximum heart output decreases, and arrhythmia (irregular beating) can occur, making exercise more difficult. Fatty deposits in and around the heart also contribute to reduced efficiency. With decreased circulation comes an increased susceptibility to cold, and an inability to regulate body temperature as efficiently as when the dog was young.

As the efficiency of the dog's cardiovascular system decreases, less oxygen is made available to the cells of the body, particularly the brain. This shortage can lead to a gradual onset of senility due to cell death caused by *anoxia,* or oxygen deprivation.

Though some cardiovascular disorders are inherited, the majority of them result from improper lifestyle habits. In general, the degeneration of your dog's cardiovascular system can be slowed down significantly, perhaps more than any other body system, just by instituting some simple lifestyle changes.

The Digestive System

Consisting of a group of organs that break down food into chemical components that your dog's body can absorb and use for energy and for building and repairing tissues, the digestive system (also known as the *alimentary tract*) is basically a tube through which food passes. Components of the digestive system include the mouth, teeth, salivary glands, tongue, throat, esophagus, stomach, intestines, liver, gall bladder, pancreas, rectum, and anus.

As your dog ages, several things occur to affect the processing of food: dental disease increases (specifically the loss or wearing away of teeth); gum disease, root abscesses, and oral tumors begin to appear more regularly; and taste sensation and salivary output is decreased. All of these changes can have a direct effect on the initial stages of food digestion and food intake. Muscles in the esophagus lose tone and do not function as effectively, making swallowing more difficult. The incidence of *gastritis,* an inflammatory condition of the stomach, increases with age, as does the appearance of gastric polyps and ulcers. The production of gastric and pancreatic secretions decreases, directly affecting the digestion of food. Liver function declines, as does the effectiveness of the intestines in digesting and absorbing nutrients and in preventing the absorption of toxins and allergens, due in part to decreased enzyme activity and chronic inflammatory damage. *Peristaltic action* (the ability of the intestines to move their contents along by muscle contraction) decreases, causing intermittent constipation. Specialized cells in the pancreas produce less insulin, raising the possibility of diabetic onset. Blood flow to all parts of the digestive system (due in part to a less efficient cardiovascular system) is diminished, further decreasing digestion. Tumors of all parts of the digestive system become more likely with age.

The actions of the digestive system, perhaps more than any other, have a profound effect on your dog's overall health and longevity. Any dog with a digestive system hampered by poor diet or lifestyle habits certainly ages at a faster rate than a pet who is optimally cared for and fed.

The Respiratory System

Consisting of the nose, larynx, sinuses, trachea, bronchial passages, and lungs, your dog's respiratory system is responsible for supplying the body with oxygen, and removing carbon dioxide and other waste gases. Perhaps reflecting aging more than any other system, the capacity and function of the respiratory system declines as much as 50 percent over the animal's life span. (This reduction in efficiency compares less favorably with the canine cardiovascular system, whose efficiency over time rarely diminishes by more than 20 or 30 percent.)

The canine respiratory system is affected in many ways by age. Especially vulnerable to various environmental factors, your dog's lungs can be damaged by pollutants such as cigarette smoke, auto emissions, and other airborne toxins, which can gradually bring on bronchitis, emphysema, carcinomas, and other diseases of the lungs. Inhaled bacteria and viruses can also lead to acute, life-threatening diseases such as pneumonia, especially if the immune system is not functioning optimally. As an animal ages, reduced numbers of *cilia*, tiny hairlike structures that help clear the air passages of mucous and other secretions, increase the chance of bronchitis and other congestive disorders. In addition, the bronchial passages tend to constrict over time, which also reduces lung capacity.

The canine lung suffers a reduced efficiency as the animal ages. In addition to a loss of capacity, the *alveoli,* tiny air sacs in the lungs responsible for diffusion of oxygen and carbon dioxide in and out of the bloodstream, suffer a decreased level of function. An increase of fibrous tissue in the lungs also occurs with age, further decreasing their effectiveness. Over time, a constrained, inefficient respiratory system places undue stress on the cardiovascular system, causing eventual heart problems. The decreased supply of oxygen that occurs with age can affect the dog's brain, eventually causing senility.

The health of your dog's respiratory system, as with all other systems, is greatly dependent on lifestyle, nutrition, and environment, three factors that are under the control of you, the owner.

The Nervous System

The nervous system of the dog consists of the brain, spinal cord, and all of the branching peripheral nerves, including those leading to the sense organs that link the body to the outside world. The brain consists of billions of nerve cells known as *neurons,* nondividing types of cells whose numbers cannot be replaced over time. The brain is the computer that coordinates all voluntary and involuntary actions in the body, allowing the dog to think, react to stimuli, and initiate her own actions.

Leading down from the brain is the spinal cord, and branching out from it to the dog's extremities are all the peripheral nerves. These peripheral nerves are separated into two categories: the *sympathetic* (voluntary) nerves and the *autonomic* (involuntary) nerves, which control automatic functions such as digestion, respiration, cardiovascular response, and the instinctive response known as "fight or flight."

As your dog ages, a gradual deterioration of the condition and number of neurons occurs, primarily due to damage resulting from free-radical reactions, which cause oxidative (free-radical) damage to the neuron's DNA and *mitochondria* (the cell structure responsible for producing the necessary energy to operate). When a neuron ceases to function, it is not replaced, unlike most other cells in the body, which are capable of division. Over time, cumulative damage to the neurons making up the nervous system leads to a loss of overall efficiency.

As neurons age, their ability to produce *neurotransmitters* decreases. These chemicals are important in allowing neurons to communicate with each other, so their reduction over time can cause your dog to suffer from a number of conditions, including: moodiness, fatigue, senility, high blood pressure, and memory loss.

As your dog's nervous system ages, her reflex actions slow. The animal takes longer to respond to stimuli, including simple commands from you, such as "sit" or "come." Older dogs often become more irritable. They also may develop involuntary tremors resulting from a decrease of the neurotransmitter *dopamine* and the continual degradation of neurons in the brain. Vision, hearing, touch, and taste all diminish with age. Curiously, a dog's sense of smell does not appear to suffer significantly, even in dogs well over twelve years of age.

The Musculoskeletal System

The muscles and bones of your dog's body work together to create movement. Contraction and flexion of a muscle cause the appendage to move within its designed range of motion. In addition, muscles allow for breathing, heartbeat, digestion, eye movement, and a host of other specialized functions. The bones, in addition to creating movement (with the help of muscles), protect internal organs, store minerals, help make blood, and give an overall framework to your dog's body.

Once a dog passes eight to ten years of age, a gradual loss of muscle mass occurs, as does a change in the size and distribution of muscle fibers. This reduction is due in part to lack of use, as well as the slow atrophy of neurons that allow the dog's brain to stimulate a muscle to contract or flex. Aging muscles also seem less able to use amino acids as a source of energy and oxygen as efficiently as when younger.

The bones of an older dog slowly begin to lose density, becoming weaker and more brittle with age, possibly due to an increasing inability of bone cells to renew themselves. As your dog ages, her activity level decreases, contributing to a further loss of bone density.

Cartilage at the ends of bones becomes weaker and thinner with age. Ligaments and tendons that connect bones to muscles also become less flexible and more fragile. The discs located between the dog's vertebrae become thinner, hence offering less cushioning than they once did, and become more likely to rupture. In addition, arthritis becomes a common problem among aging canines. Breaks, fractures, muscle pulls, and ligament and tendon tears also are more likely.

The Skin and Hair

Also known as the *integumentary system,* the skin and hair of your dog serves a vital role in maintaining health. In addition to acting as a barrier to infection, your dog's skin regulates body temperature (though not as profoundly as in humans), prevents dehydration, and acts as a large sense organ. Hair acts as an insulator, keeping your dog warm in cool climates, as well as acting as a protective layer for the skin.

As a dog passes seven or eight years of age, her hair begins to be duller and drier. Due to decreased follicular activity, *alopecia* (hair loss) can occur in random areas. A graying of the hairs around the muzzle is common after seven or eight years of age, and can occur in other areas as the dog continues to age.

Canine skin becomes somewhat less pliable with age, as a result of becoming thinner, due in part to an increase in calcium within the elastic fibers, as well as a gradual destruction of connective tissue components. Calluses often form over pressure points, particularly the elbows. Glands in the skin function less efficiently, and cysts can occur. Older dogs have an increased occurrence of skin tumors, and tend to be more susceptible to skin allergies and particularly to fleas. Therapies exist to prevent skin disorders and to adjust the diet.

The Endocrine System

Composed of "ductless" glands that secrete hormones into the bloodstream, your dog's endocrine system profoundly influences metabolism. Hormones are used by the body to control a variety of functions and behaviors essential to the well-being of your dog. For instance, the hormone *adrenaline,* produced by the adrenal glands, floods the dog's system in order to provoke a rapid response, perhaps necessary during a life-threatening fight-or-flight situation. And the hormone *estrogen,* produced by the ovaries, controls the timing of ovulation and breeding behavior in the female dog.

With increased age comes a pronounced decrease in the secretion of hormones, particularly by the thymus, thyroid, testes, and ovaries. Reasons for these changes vary from gland to gland, and can include cell death or atrophy, increased production of fibrous or fatty tissues within each gland, cysts or tumor growth, or even autoimmune attacks on the glands. Numerous approaches are available to maintain the health of your dog's endocrine system, including exercise, diet, neutering, and nutritional therapies.

The Immune System

Your dog's immune system protects her from the invasion of foreign bodies that could harm or weaken her. Her immune system recognizes all types of body tissues and substances that "belong," and attempts to quarantine and destroy anything that doesn't. Bacteria, viruses, foreign proteins, chemicals, allergens, and even cancer cells are attacked, destroyed, or excreted.

Your dog's immune system is comprised of the spleen, thymus gland, bone marrow, and lymphatic system, which includes the lymph nodes. The bone marrow manufacture *leukocytes* (or white blood cells), which are the main attack force of the immune system and appear in numerous forms. Once mature, leukocytes travel to various areas of the dog's body, according to their "preprogrammed" function. Some are found in the lymphatic fluids and some in various organs such as the liver, while others continually circulate in the blood.

Biochemical messaging involving various types of leukocytes and the brain controls the actions of the immune system. These chemical messages dictate the type of "battle" that a dog's immune system wages against its perceived enemies. These "foes" appear constantly and pervasively: Countless millions of invaders attack your dog's body each day—and are routinely disposed of by her healthy immune system. (*Antibodies,* types of proteins manufactured by specific types of white cells, seek out, attack, and neutralize *antigens,* the foreign proteins contained in bacteria, bacterial toxins, viruses, and other toxins such as pollutants, which effectively destroy the invaders.)

Antibodies also can be formed in response to the introduction of a vaccine, providing immunity against a known and potentially life-threatening infection, such as rabies. The antibody produced by the lymphocyte fits perfectly into the antigen, much the same way that only one key fits the right lock, making identification of that contaminant simple and effective. Once antibodies to a specific antigen are produced, they remain in the dog's system for years, protecting her from future infection. This immunity factor is normally many times more effective than it needs to be in a healthy dog. This redundancy or "reserve factor" is a vitally important ingredient in maintaining your dog's health and extending her life span.

As your dog ages, however, her immune system begins to lose its effectiveness and its reserve capacity, resulting in an increasing vulnerability to attack from foreign invaders. Organs of the immune system produce fewer and less effective leukocytes, thus increasing the chances of infections or cancer. In addition to this lowered resistance, the immune system of an aged or sick dog can sometimes go haywire and attack the body's own tissues, resulting in serious autoimmune disorders such as rheumatoid arthritis, thyroid disease, and kidney disease.

A variety of therapies may bolster the effectiveness of the aging dog's immune system, including nutritional and herbal supplementation that can increase the dog's functional reserves, by increasing the production of leukocytes, antibodies, and antioxidants

The Urinary System

Consisting of the kidneys, ureter, bladder, and urethra, the urinary system is responsible for filtering and removing wastes, toxins, and excess water from your dog's body. It also helps maintain an acidic base and electrolyte balance. The urinary system is vitally important, and though resilient, it can eventually lose its effectiveness as your dog ages. A gradual decline in kidney weight and function normally occurs in the aging dog, as does a decrease in blood flow to the kidneys, leading to atrophy and an increase in nonfunctional fibrous tissue growth. The kidney's ability to filter toxins from the blood decreases, resulting in a higher percentage of toxic material in the body. Cysts, stones, and infections become more common in the bladder as a result of incomplete emptying. Incontinence can also occur, particularly while the older dog sleeps. Tumors of the kidneys and bladder occur more frequently.

Various therapies are designed to maintain and improve the efficiency of your dog's urinary system, including close monitoring of diet and water intake, reduction of toxins, proper regulation of

sodium and protein intake, exercise, and vitamin and herbal supplementation designed to optimize kidney function.

The degeneration of the various systems in your dog's body collec-
tively contributes to the aging process. If slowing down the degenerative process in any *one* of these systems can increase the life
span of your pet, just think what effect slowing the degeneration of
all the systems could have! The therapies discussed in this book are
intended to help you accomplish this, resulting in a longer, more
satisfying relationship between you and your pet. The next section
contains a detailed, step-by-step outline of a six-point plan that will
enable you to care effectively for your dog's health and improve the
quality of her life as well. Read on, and then give them a try. You
won't be sorry.

PART II

Understanding the Plan: Step-by-Step Explanations

Step 1. Stay in Touch with Your Dog's Health

Subtle signs of an impending illness in your dog often can be detected well ahead of more advanced, serious, and obvious symptoms. By staying in touch with your dog's appearance and behavior on a daily basis, you are far better able to detect the subtle beginnings of an illness, disorder, or disease, many of which can significantly shorten your pet's life span if not discovered early enough.

Having a capable and caring veterinarian in your corner is another valuable asset in maintaining your dog's good health and preventing life-shortening illnesses. Developing a good working relationship—in effect, a partnership—with your veterinarian ensures that your dog has several concerned and informed eyes looking out for him. Read on to learn how to become intimately familiar with your dog's ideal physical and psychological condition so that you can quickly recognize any deviation, however subtle, as a possible vanguard of illness or systemic weakness (that leads to illness). Promptly sharing any pertinent information with your veterinarian may be helpful in the early diagnosis and treatment of a disorder that, left untreated, could shorten your dog's life.

The Weekly Home Exam:
Recognize Early Signs of Illness

Once each week, spend 10 or 15 minutes examining your dog from head to toe to ensure that he appears healthy and normal. As you become intimately familiar with your dog's outward appearance, abnormalities that you once might not have noticed now become obvious to you. Paying attention to each part of your dog's body on a weekly basis will cue you in to any subtle changes that denote possible encroaching illness. The weekly home exam teaches you to appreciate your dog's normal appearance and behavior so that you can have a background against which to recognize abnormal developments.

THE COAT

The condition of your dog's coat can be a great indicator of his general health. A dry, dull, thinning coat, or one with excessive hair loss, can point to a variety of health problems, including allergies, nutritional deficiencies, hormonal imbalances, parasites, underlying infection, or excess stress and anxiety. Each of these problems, if left untreated, can significantly shorten your dog's life span.

At least once each week, check your dog's coat closely. Is it shiny and lustrous, or dull and thin? Look for thinning or patchy spots and get a general sense of its luster. Make a note of overly dry or greasy hair, bare spots, scabs, pimples, redness, rawness, fleas, or unpleasant odors (which could indicate a skin infection), then mention them to your vet.

After looking the coat over, go ahead and give your dog a good brushing from head to toe, even if his coat is a short one. In addition to being healthy and enjoyable for your pet, brushing helps you make a mental map of every inch of his coat, allowing you to accurately compare your observations each week. The physical contact also helps the two of you bond and desensitizes your dog to the prolonged touch that is essential to any thorough examination process.

THE SKIN

While brushing your dog's coat, be sure to closely examine his skin, which is often hard to see clearly, particularly with thick-coated breeds like sheepdogs or huskies. Overly dry or flaky skin, pimples, open sores, parasites, or unusual secretions are all indicative of significant problems, so contact your vet if you detect any of these. Check for lumps, which can indicate cysts, infection, injury, or tumorous growths. Be aware of redness or irritation, and pay attention to any scratching, biting, or excessive licking your dog does to specific areas, which may indicate parasites, particularly fleas. Scabs, pus, unusual discolorations, or abnormally sensitive areas all point to health problems that could require medical attention, or at least a change in diet or lifestyle. Minor scrapes or abrasions are often the result of playful activities in the home and yard. They will generally heal on their own. Observe such minor injuries—if they progressively improve over a five-day period, no veterinary care is required.

THE EYES

Look closely into your dog's eyes. Are they shiny and clear-looking, with no bloodshot areas in the white portions? Or are they dull, bloodshot, inflamed, or clouded? Is your dog squinting or afraid of bright light? A dog's eye can suffer from scratches or abrasions to its *cornea* (the transparent surface), cataracts, infection, ingrown eyelashes, or turned-in lids (known as *entropion*). Are the pupils the same size? Check for any unusual tearing or mucous discharge in the inner corner of the eyes. Older dogs may suffer from a progressively cloudy, degenerative lens condition known as a cataract, which could require surgery if it becomes serious enough to reduce your dog's vision. A red, inflamed eye can be caused by many different stimuli including glaucoma, which is the most serious and requires immediate attention.

THE NOSE

Your dog's nose can be called normal whether it is warm or cold, moist or dry. An overly dry or warm nose could indicate an illness or infection, so be aware of this—and be familiar with what is normal for your dog. Any unusual discharge from your dog's nostrils could point to a respiratory infection, allergy, or other upper-respiratory disorder, so report this to your vet as soon as possible.

THE EARS

Look into your dog's ears closely, checking for any excess wax buildup, dirt, pus, foreign bodies or inflammation. Any of these problems could point to a bacterial infection, yeast infection, or parasitic infestation, allergy, injury, or imbedded foreign body, so be aware of this. In addition to looking in the ears, pay attention to any unpleasant odor that could be indicative of infection or dirt buildup. Be sure to check the skin on the outside of his ears. Report any abnormality to your vet as soon as possible. (A normal ear is odorless and contains little or no dirt or wax, the skin on the inner side of the ear is smooth and white-to-light-pink in color.)

THE MOUTH

Look into your dog's mouth and check the condition of his gums, teeth, tongue, and palate. The gums should be pink and moist, not pale and dry-looking. Check for gum inflammation, especially along the teeth margin, and note pus discharge, discoloration, or bleeding. The teeth should appear white and properly aligned, with little or no tartar buildup or cavities. Look for broken or chipped teeth, which may eventually lead to a root abscess and can ultimately result in a very painful condition and the loss of the tooth. The tongue should be pink and moist (some breeds, like the Chow, have a dark gray tongue), not dry and coated. Dark-colored areas on the tongue, gums, lips, or palate are common and do not necessarily indicate poor health, but be aware of any masses that appear or grow suddenly. Check for any foreign bodies stuck in the teeth, gums, or palate, which could lead to infection and pain. Also check for retention of baby teeth, which are smaller, thinner, sharper and more delicate—they should be lost by 8 months of age. Any retained baby teeth should be extracted by your vet.

THE FEET

Healthy feet are important to any dog's well-being, and thus need to be checked closely for any abnormalities that could affect walking or running. When a dog favors a foot because of an injured toe, pad, nail, or broken bone, he begins to alter the physical stress placed on the bones of the legs, shoulders, and back, leading to eventual chronic structural problems.

Check all pads on your dog's feet. They should be firm and durable, with a somewhat callused feel to them, but without significant cracking or scaling. Look for tears or imbedded foreign objects such as thorns or glass shards. Any rawness or wound should be brought to your vet's attention. Next, check the nails, which should be kept short enough to avoid making contact with the ground when the dog is standing. Fractured or scaly nails could indicate a dietary deficiency, dehydration, or fungal infection. Nails allowed to grow too long can cause improper foot placement, leading to toe, ankle, shoulder, or hip problems. See Step 2, pp. 66–67, for nail-trimming directions. After examining the nails, quickly look over the top of each foot, checking for any cuts, swelling, or other abnormalities which, if present for more than four or five days, would necessitate a call to your vet. Handle each foot, checking to see if there is any pain reaction to applied pressure. Also, be sure to look between the toes for redness or imbedded objects such as thorns, foxtails, stones, or salt.

THE LIMBS

After examining your dog's feet, look over each leg carefully. His legs are his means of locomotion; without the ability to walk or run, your dog's life would be seriously threatened. Dogs who lose most or *all* leg mobility are more often than not put to sleep, so always be thorough when examining the legs.

Moving up from the feet, gently work the ankle joint or wrist, checking for any pain or discomfort, which could indicate a sprain, break, soft-tissue injury, or the onset of arthritis (in an older dog). Massage up each leg, again checking for any pain or discomfort as evidenced by a sudden yelp or struggle. Holding each front leg at the ankle joint, work the leg so that the elbow and shoulder (or knee and pelvis, in the case of a rear leg) are put through a full range of motion. Any discomfort could point to injury or the onset of arthritis, so be sure to let your vet know as soon as possible.

In addition to physically examining the legs themselves, pay attention to your dog's gait. Report any limping or imbalance to your vet. Also note if there is any substantial size differential with regard to bone thickness and muscularity; if present, it could point to a neural, circulatory, or disuse problem. If injury or disease has left a limb less capable, the dog may not use it as much, resulting in atrophy.

THE BACK

As with humans, the health of a dog's back is crucial to his overall well-being. Luckily for them, dogs do not stand upright on two legs, and therefore have fewer problems than do bipeds like ourselves. Injuries or arthritis can occur, however, especially in the older dog, as can ruptures of the *discs,* the shock-absorbing "pillows" found between the vertebrae. An injured back should be brought to the attention of your vet as soon as possible, as any trauma to the enclosed spinal cord can result in partial or total paralysis.

While your dog is standing, simply massage up his back—on

either side of the vertebrae from the hips to the head—using a firm rotating motion of the fingers, checking for any signs of discomfort during the procedure. Also, feel for any areas that seem swollen or overly warm to the touch, a sign indicating that injury or infection could be present. Then, with your dog still standing, push straight down over the shoulder blades and then over the pelvis, again checking for any discomfort. Make sure to be more gentle with a small or aged dog, and bit firmer with a larger breed. Last, gently feel each vertebrae in the dog's tail, checking for any kinks, pain, or injury. Be especially observant of possible wounds from fighting with other animals, as the tail seems to get bitten more often than other areas of the body. Any signs of pain during the exam could point to injury, arthritis, hip dysplasia, or other problems, so report them to your vet as soon as possible.

THE CHEST AND ABDOMINAL AREAS

Pain in either one of these areas could indicate injury or gastrointestinal disorders, such as bloat. With your dog standing, place an open hand on his breastbone and press up gently but steadily, checking for any discomfort. Move your hands to each side of his rib cage and press inward, again watching for any pain reaction. Then, with your dog still standing, gently hold the abdomen between thumbs and fingers, push up, and squeeze gently. If the dog shows pain or the area seems tense, swollen, extremely rigid, or warm to the touch, see your vet as soon as possible.

THE RECTAL AND GENITAL AREAS

Inflammation or unusual discharge from these areas can point to infection or illness, so always give each area a careful visual exam. Check for pus, blood, swelling, or excess dirt, as well as fecal or urine leakage, which are more likely to occur in the older dog. Also, check for signs of any parasites, especially worms, in the rectal area. (In particular, pieces of tapeworm often can be found adhering to the rectal area of an infested dog.) If found, see your vet, who can rid your pet of these health-sapping pests through the use of oral medication. Observe your dog as he defecates and urinates, and make note of excessive straining. Look for swelling or tenderness at the 4 and 8 o'clock position around your pet's anus. Any distension or sensitivity could be evidence that the anal glands are full—especially if your dog licks the rectal area frequently or drags his rear end along the ground. This will require your veterinarian to manually squeeze the fluid from the sacs. This is not something to attempt at home. It must be done by a veterinary professional.

THE LYMPH NODES

You can check your dog's lymph nodes by becoming familiar with their positioning and their normal size and shape. You'll find them under the angle of the lower jaw, just in front of the shoulder blade on each side of the neck, in the armpit area, in the groin area, and behind the knees. After you examine them, note any enlargement or change in shape and report these to your vet if these changes persist.

The Vital Signs: Know What's Normal

In addition to performing the weekly home physical exam, you should also take weekly measurements of your dog's vital signs, including:

WEIGHT

Be sure to keep track of your dog's weight on a monthly basis. Any significant change (10 percent or more) up or down could indicate illness, improper diet, parasitic infection, thyroid disease, or dehydration, so make sure not to lose sight of this important indicator. Obesity can predispose your pet to diabetes, musculoskeletal problems, heart disease, and cancer. On the other hand, underweight dogs may suffer from a host of disorders related to malnutrition. The older dog may have a propensity to gain weight or may become more finicky at mealtime, which makes weighing the aging animal regularly even more important.

Dogs under 50 or 60 pounds can simply be picked up in their owner's arms and weighed on the bathroom scale along with the owner, who can then subtract his or her own weight to arrive at the dog's true weight. For dogs over 60 pounds, either find a friend strong enough to do the lifting or make a monthly trip to the vet's office to use his or her walk-on scale. Using two people and two scales also works. Short of actually weighing your dog, you can "eyeball" his body during the weekly exam and also feel how much fat is overlaid atop the rib cage. When using gentle pressure, if you cannot feel the line of your dog's ribs, chances are he is overweight. If his ribs stick out prominently, your pet is probably underweight.

RESPIRATION

A dog's normal rate of breathing varies quite a bit depending on his size and level of activity. Generally speaking, your dog's resting respiration rate should be anywhere from 10 to 20 breaths per minute, 10 for a large dog and 20 for a small dog (puppies will breathe somewhat faster due to their smaller size). With anxiety or added activity, this number will increase substantially. Departure from this resting range could indicate overheating, lung or heart disease, stress, pain, injury, obesity, or a number of other serious metabolic problems. The older dog's respiration rate is more apt to increase, particularly if he is suffering from any of the just-mentioned disorders. Dogs left in hot automobiles without adequate ventilation or water increase their respiration rates precipitously in an attempt to cool off. *This very dangerous habit of leaving dogs in the car should be avoided,* especially with the older or smaller dog, neither being able to regulate body temperature as well as a younger, larger animal.

To measure your dog's respiration, simply count his breaths over a 30-second interval, then multiply by 2 to get the number of breaths per minute. If you are not sure what "normal" should be for your dog, ask your vet.

Also get an impression of the depth and smoothness of each respiration. If the respirations are unusually deep or jerky and labored compared with what you commonly see, and this pattern continues, contact your vet. Shallow, rapid respirations may also be a concern.

PULSE/HEART BEAT

Your dog's resting pulse can be a good indicator of his overall health. A weak rapid pulse could point to a heart problem of some sort, as can an erratic one. Checking the pulse is especially important with an older dog, who is more susceptible to cardiovascular or respiratory disease. Any dog who is ill or pregnant should also have his or her heart rate and/or pulse checked regularly.

Choose a time of day when your dog is sedate and quiet. Then, with your dog lying down on one side, measure the heart rate and rhythm. Place your hand underneath his front leg where it meets the chest, and rest your palm at that spot on the chest. You can measure the pulse, as opposed to the heart beat, by placing your hand flat over the inside of the back leg (inner thigh), just below where the leg meets the abdomen. Wait until you can feel a pulse, then count it off for 15 seconds and multiply by 4 to arrive at the correct number of beats per minute. A normal resting heart rate should measure anywhere between 70 and 120 beats per minute, depending on the size of the dog. Be sure to ask your vet just what your dog's ideal resting pulse should be, in order to have an idea of how your dog is doing. Anything outside of the prescribed range, especially for an older dog, should be reported to your vet as soon as possible. Be sure to gain a sense of the strength and rhythm of the pulse as well as the rate.

TEMPERATURE

Your dog's normal resting body temperature should measure between 100.5°F and 101.5°F. Variations may occur from dog to dog
and day to day according to size and previous level of activity. Unusually low or high body temperature can be indicative of a number
of life-shortening problems, including infection, thyroid abnormalities, hypo- or hyperthermia, or numerous other metabolic disorders.
Obtain an accurate, digital thermometer made of plastic from
your local pet shop or drugstore. Traditional glass thermometers
filled with mercury are potentially dangerous when used on dogs, as
they can break and cause injury or poisoning, especially with a pan-
icked or uncooperative animal. Though more expensive, the digital
plastic thermometers are safer and more accurate.

With your dog standing or lying on his side, slowly insert the
clean, well-lubricated thermometer far enough into the dog's rectum
to register correctly, which is usually about 1 inch. If necessary,
have a friend help keep your dog still and calm. Wait at least 1
minute before removing the thermometer (or just wait for the beep if
it's digital), then check the reading. If the results are outside the
normal parameters, contact your vet as soon as possible.

BLOOD PRESSURE AND STATE OF HYDRATION

You can get a sense of your dog's blood pressure by using finger
pressure to cause the color of the gums to blanch. Color should return within 1–2 seconds after removing your finger. If the gums cap-
illary refill time is much longer than 2 seconds it could indicate low
blood pressure, so contact your vet.

You can acquire a vague sense of your dog's state of hydration by
checking his skin's elasticity. Using your thumb and forefinger,
grasp and lift a small amount of skin—then let it go and see how
quickly it settles back to normal—this should occur almost immediately if hydration is normal and skin elasticity is good.

Keeping a Medical Log

After measuring your dog's physiological signs, record them in a notebook that will act as your dog's medical log. Doing so will provide you with a long-running record, helpful in revealing long-term trends in your dog's health. For instance, you are most likely to notice a slight seasonal rise in respiration rates during the warmer summer months, as well as a slightly higher pulse rate due to increased respiration and activity levels. Weight is most likely to increase during the winter and decrease during more-active summer months. If upon reviewing your dog's medical log, you see an unexpected pattern forming, you may want to bring it to the attention of your vet. For instance, a steady drop in weight over a 6-month period combined with rising pulse and respiration rates could indicate an infection, a heart problem, or some type of metabolic disorder. The medical log should also keep track of any unusual observations on the weekly exam, including any tenderness, sensitivity, or appearance of fleas, growths, or abnormal looking teeth. When going to the vet for your dog's annual checkup, bring the log with you and show it to him or her. It could be an indispensable tool in discovering a hidden disease in its very early stages, which could save your pet's life.

In addition to familiarizing yourself with your dog's physical appearance, you should pay close attention to his behavior on a daily basis. Any significant changes could indicate a hidden illness; being aware of your dog's moods and habits are a key to catching problems before they become serious. For example, a good eater who suddenly becomes finicky at dinnertime could be suffering from an illness that so far has no other symptoms. Likewise, a happy, sociable animal who gradually becomes listless and isolated could be suffering from a disorder or injury that, if not discovered early, could threaten his or her life.

When making note of your dog's day-to-day behavior, be aware of any marked changes from his normal routine. Outgoing dogs who suddenly become shy or worried, active dogs who become sedentary, or dogs with a dramatically increased thirst or sleep time could all be showing signs that point to a brewing medical problem. Also watch your dog when he urinates or defecates; if he seems to be straining or in pain, call your vet. Paying attention to your pet's behavior and making note of it in your medical log may one day save his life.

Psychological and Physiological
Symptoms to Look For

Any behavior that is out of the ordinary for your dog
Unusual lethargy or hyperactivity
Exhaustion
Modified sleep patterns
Depression, moodiness, or irritability
Aggression toward other animals or persons
Extreme territoriality
Panting, salivating, whining, or pacing
Diarrhea, constipation, or incontinence
Painful or difficult urination
Profound changes in appetite or thirst
Loss of balance or coordination
Changes in depth and rhythm of respiration or heartbeat
Sudden disobedience
Uncharacteristic barking or silence
Limping
Vomiting or regurgitating
Coughing, gagging, sneezing, or wheezing
Excessive scratching or rubbing
Scooting or biting at anus
Head-shaking or scratching at ears
Squinting
Change in posture, head carriage, foot placement, or overall gait
Lumps, bumps, scabs on skin, hair loss, or dull coat

Finding the Best Veterinarian

Selecting a veterinarian for your dog could be one of the most important steps in helping him to live the longest, healthiest life possible. At some time, your dog may require expert medical attention to save his life; you will want the right vet there, deciding just what needs to be done. So it's wise to know how to select a competent, caring vet.

First, consider the qualities that are important to you. Would you prefer a vet who sticks to purely conventional methods or one who utilizes some alternative therapies in conjunction with traditional, time-honored techniques? Consider the vet's philosophy; does he or she emphasize preventive medicine, or just a straightforward diagnostic approach, treating a dog only after illness or injury has appeared? Does he or she believe in helping you determine the right diet for your dog, or simply leave that up to you? These qualities are personal choices that you should make according to your own philosophy and expectations. If a vet's approach does not come close to mirroring your own views, consider continuing the search. Do the two of you get along well? Are there "good vibes"?

One important issue with regard to choosing a vet is convenience. No one wants to travel more than 20 minutes or so to get to the veterinary clinic, especially when a dog is seriously ill. Ideally, choose a clinic located no more than 5 to 10 miles from your home. Also, make sure the clinic's hours of operation fit your schedule.

Next, make sure that the vet you choose provides accessible emergency-care facilities for his or her clients. A medical crisis rarely occurs at a convenient time, so having a late-night emergency service available could save your pet's life. Most vets either provide this service themselves, or refer clients to a capable emergency clinic nearby. Some even give out their home phone number.

Any veterinarian service you choose should be well organized and professionally operated. The facility should appear clean and orderly, and have a large enough waiting room to keep owners and their various pets separated from each other, in order to prevent aggression or the spread of disease. The office should honor your appointment time as closely as is possible, and the mood of the place should be one of calm, not stress. Avoid any clinic with a rude, uncaring staff.

The vet you choose should be easy to talk to and eager to listen to your opinions and desires. Some vets, though skilled at their craft, do not communicate all that well with people. A vet simply must be a good communicator, and be able to explain a situation and course of action to a concerned owner, without becoming patronizing or impatient. Avoid a vet who seems rude or easily annoyed by reasonable questions. If you do not feel at ease with the vet's personality, find someone else.

Always choose a vet who allows you to be present during simple diagnostic or therapeutic procedures. This helps keep your dog calm, and is a great learning opportunity for you. A confident, caring vet should not mind you watching him or her examining your pet or drawing his blood.

A quality vet always attempts to expand his or her knowledge by reading the latest medical studies, attending seminars, and pursuing other paths of continuing education and training.

Make sure your vet is reasonably priced given the time and expertise he or she provides. Paying a higher fee for a more thorough, careful exam may prove less expensive in the long run. A clinic that is well equipped and hires a caring and careful staff is worth paying more for. Avoid low-cost, high-volume clinics, which sometimes lack experienced vets and quality care. Although cost should not be the sole criterion for selecting a vet, many people do consider it during the selection process.

Where does one begin to look for this perfect vet? The best method is often the simplest and most time-tested; ask friends or relatives if they are happy with their vets. If they are, consider giving one of their vets a try. A referral from someone who you trust is often a reliable way to find a competent professional, so consider listening to those you know and trust.

You may give your local county vet association a call and ask them if they can recommend a good vet. The shelter or breeder from whom you obtained your dog can probably put you in touch with a competent veterinarian in your area. Also, try contacting other local animal professionals and ask them whom they use. Canine trainers, groomers, or breeders can often suggest someone who they consider to be a great vet.

Don't be afraid to respond to advertisements in the Yellow Pages or another publication. Though you won't learn much from the ad, you will be able to compile a list of possible choices. Contact each to get a feel for how things are run. Try to visit as many as possible. Make sure to talk briefly with the vet to determine if he or she is personable and helpful. You may also want to ask about the range of services provided (e.g., boarding or grooming) and the hours of operation. It also helps to know how long the vet has been in practice, and whether he or she has areas of special interest or an affinity for certain breeds.

Utilizing a Vet

Once you have chosen a veterinarian, you should learn how to best utilize his or her skills in order to provide your dog with the best possible health care. Developing a good working relationship with a vet is one of the keys to extending your dog's life. It's best, then, to start out on the right foot.

From the time you first adopt or buy your dog right through to his old age, you should make sure to schedule an annual, if not a semi-annual checkup, even when all seems normal to you. Remember that the absence of symptoms does not necessarily mean good health, but only that no overt signs of disease or illness are currently apparent to you. Many life-shortening conditions can develop that do not express themselves until substantial damage has been done. Certain types of cancer are an example of this, as are diabetes, heart disease, and progressive kidney failure. Your vet, by carefully performing an examination and routine blood, fecal, and urine tests, is able to detect many life-shortening conditions, which, if caught in time, may be cured or minimized, or their progression slowed.

The annual checkup gives you a great opportunity to learn about veterinary medicine, and allows you to pick up tips on preventive medicine, nutrition, grooming, and hands-on homecare techniques, such as taking your dog's temperature, pulse, or clipping his nails. Your vet can give you invaluable advice on how to maintain a safe, toxin-free environment, and may even be able to help you handle behavioral problems. If you watch him or her carefully examine your dog, you also can pick up tips on how to give a home physical.

When you take your dog in to the vet for his annual checkup, be prepared to answer these basic questions that may be posed to you by the veterinarian:

- Do you have any major concerns or have you noticed any symptoms regarding your dog's health? If so, when did they begin, how did they progress, and in what order did they occur?
- Have you noticed any unusual behavioral problems or symptoms? If so, when did they first appear, how did they progress, in what order did they appear, and what kind of home treatment (if any) have you given?
- How is your dog's appetite, thirst, elimination habits, and overall demeanor? What does his diet consist of? What is the color, shape, consistency, and volume of his stool? Does he urinate and defecate without straining? What is the color of the urine?

What To Expect from an Exam

The actual exam done by your vet is a procedure that—although very basic—to be done properly, takes years to master. Palpating and evaluating bones, muscles, joints, and internal organs, as well as listening closely to the heart and lungs, are skills that vets continually strive to perfect as they examine each new patient. Learning to recognize subtle changes in behavior and finding ways to discover where a dog hurts require a special talent and years of practice.

First, your vet studies your dog's history, which may provide more important information than the exam itself. Therefore, try to provide your vet with as accurate and detailed a history as possible, so his job as a "health detective" is easier. Next, the vet discusses your dog's diet with you and offers suggestions for changes if necessary. The dog's weight is taken, to determine if the animal is at his proper weight. If overweight, the vet will recommend a diet and exercise program that suits your pet. Then, a complete physical is done, which is similar to but more thorough and professional than the home exam mentioned earlier. If your pet has any abnormality, chances are your vet will detect it. Vital signs are measured, and fecal, urine, and blood samples are often taken for testing to determine if any internal abnormalities are present. In effect, all the dog's systems are inspected and evaluated. If anything out of the ordinary is found, the vet discusses a course of action with you that hopefully puts your dog back on the track to good health.

Visiting the vet at least once each year helps keep your vet familiarized with your dog. Remember that he or she sees hundreds of pets each year; waiting too long between visits only serves to reduce the level of doctor-patient relationship. Realize that, to a vet, your dog is a unique individual and a cared-for patient—not just a statistic. Any good doctor, whether treating human or animal clients, wants to relate to the patient on an intimate level. By knowing your dog's personality and temperament, your vet is better able to detect behavioral changes that might help with diagnosis or prevention.

In preparation for your dog's visit to the vet, make sure to handle and examine your pet on a regular basis, so he is desensitized to manipulation and touch, two things that definitely happen at the vet's office. Many owners rarely if ever handle their dog's feet or legs, look in their mouths, or take their temperatures, leaving this up to the vet, who must then deal with a stubborn, resistant dog who may react defensively to close examination. To avoid this, regularly handle your dog. Brush him, clip his nails, clean his ears and teeth, bathe him, and take his temperature. (See Step 2 for grooming tips, pp. 62–68.) Doing these things consistently from early on in your dog's life ensures an easier time for the vet *and* your pet when exam time comes around.

As an added plus, daily handling of your dog helps you detect abnormalities, such as lumps, rashes, wounds, parasites, broken teeth, hair loss, or sensitive areas. Finding a problem in advance saves your vet time and could save your dog's life. Owners who do not regularly handle their dogs are much less likely to detect problems early on. Catching a problem in its early stages could reduce your vet fees and result in a significant extension of your canine friend's time here with you.

Be polite and respectful to your vet, and try to develop a good working rapport. Be on time for your appointment and respect his or her hours. Learn to trust him or her, which helps to ensure the best treatment possible for your pet. Do, however, require your vet to adequately explain a condition or treatment to you in clear, understandable terms, so you aren't left feeling confused and distrustful. Don't be afraid to ask pertinent questions; your vet appreciates you showing interest and involvement. And don't be afraid to disagree if you feel strongly about something, provided you have carefully weighed the options and have asked the right questions. Remember, you spend more time with your dog than the vet does, and therefore may be more aware of his normal behavior and have a sense of when something is just not right. If necessary, obtain a second opinion if your vet suggests a course of action with which you feel uncomfortable. That said, do give your vet a chance to explain the rationale behind his advice before seeking other opinions.

Make sure to provide the vet with a detailed background/history of your dog, including where he was obtained. Shelter or pet-shop

dogs often suffer from parasitic infestations, bite wounds, gastrointestinal problems, or stress-related disorders. Dogs obtained from a
quality breeder usually experience fewer disorders due to better
overall care. Let your vet know if any hereditary or congenital problems exist with your dog or any of his line. Knowing if a sibling or
parent suffers from a chronic condition such as heart arrhythmia,
diabetes, or hip dysplasia aids your vet in searching for answers to
your dog's health problems.

Any allergies, fluctuations in weight, respiration, pulse, or behavior should be reported as well, as this is all pertinent to a proper
diagnosis. Be sure to include information on diet and exercise, any
previous treatments done by other vets, and any medications or supplements you are giving. Overall, being helpful, attentive, and curious with your vet greatly increases his or her ability to help your
dog, thereby extending your pet's time with you and your family.

Step 2. Ensure Exercise, Grooming, and Dental Hygiene

A dog who is physically fit and hygienically sound has a much better chance of living a longer, fuller, healthier life than one who is unkempt and out of shape. Like yourself, your dog needs to regularly participate in some form of aerobic activity in order to stay fit, toned, and close to her ideal weight. An active, fit dog's cardiovascular and respiratory systems degenerate far more slowly with age than those of a sedentary, obese animal. Overall, exercise is a miraculous yet easy way of extending your beloved pet's life.

A dog who is infrequently bathed, brushed, or checked for parasites suffers more frequent bouts of skin and coat disorders and infections than a dog who receives regular grooming attention. The unkempt dog forced to endure unclean conditions for long periods of time ultimately has her entire system taxed, particularly her immune system, which is forced to deal with skin rashes, fleas, worms, bacteria, and other irritants to her coat and skin. A well-groomed dog suffers less stress, allowing her immune system and antioxidant defense system, in particular, to maintain a higher "reserve," which is useful in combating more serious illnesses that may beset the dog.

In addition to keeping your dog well-groomed and parasite-free, you should consider the important role that dental hygiene plays in maintaining good health. The health of a dog's teeth and gums are vitally important to the health of her heart, lungs, kidney, and liver, as a healthy mouth is a prerequisite for good digestion. Bacteria that feed, breed, and multiply in the plaque that forms on the teeth produce toxins. Both bacteria and toxins can enter the bloodstream and eventually injure internal organs. Maintaining good dental hygiene is, therefore, another key ingredient in giving your animal the best possible chance at living a long and happy life.

Exercise

Regular activity is an essential ingredient in a healthy dog's day. Physical activities such as running, walking, jumping, and playing work the muscles, strengthen the heart and lungs, increase circulation, raise overall metabolism, and prevent excess weight gain. The tissues of an active dog's body receive nutrients, blood, and oxygen more readily, which helps with new cell growth, dead cell removal, digestion, and immune-system response time. Regular exercise lowers resting blood pressure and pulse rate, and helps cleanse the body of any toxins. By regulating weight, exercise helps prevent disorders such as cancer, diabetes, heart disease, arthritis, and joint disorders that are worsened by obesity. In addition, regular vigorous activity helps strengthen the muscles and bones, which can become porous and brittle later in life (particularly in the lethargic dog).

No matter what breed or size of dog you have, some form of daily exercise is possible. Certain breeds, particularly hunting or herding dogs, take to exercise naturally, as their original jobs required them to be very active for extended periods. Labradors, pointers, Border collies, greyhounds, and Siberian huskies are a few examples of breeds who are easy to motivate, as are mixed-breed dogs with any of these breeds in their bloodlines. Taking your dog for a jog, run, swim, or long walk, or teaching her to retrieve a Frisbee or tennis ball, are perfect ways to work her muscles, joints, heart, and lungs. Smaller, more sedate lapdogs such as Chihuahuas, Maltese, toy poodles, or Pomeranians can still be played with, taken out for a daily walk, and even taught to retrieve a favorite toy in the home. No matter which type of dog you have, you can find some activity she enjoys. And make sure it is something that both of you can participate in, making it more interesting for your dog and also helpful in strengthening the human-animal bond.

Older, slower dogs and larger, heavier breeds benefit from some form of daily exercise, but should not be expected to participate at the same level of intensity as younger, more lithe animals. For instance, a 9-year-old overweight Saint Bernard should not be taken for vigorous runs, particularly during warm, humid conditions, as this could do more harm than good. The same dog, though, unless arthritic, certainly benefits from a 30-minute brisk walk 2 or 3 times each day, combined with some dietary adjustments to help bring down her weight.

Older dogs and those with joint problems should never be pushed too hard or long; shorter, easier, more frequent exercise is more appropriate. And, like the larger, heavier dogs, older animals should never be expected or encouraged to jump off of high objects or over fences, as this increases the risk of muscle pulls, tendon tears, fractures, and injuries to the hips, back, and shoulders.

Exercises that you may heartily encourage your dog to participate in include:

- Fetching a toy
- Walking, jogging, or running with you, or running next to you while biking (stay away from busy streets where breathing car engine fumes may more than negate the benefits of jogging)
- Swimming
- Hiking
- Herding
- Agility competitions, fly-ball competition
- Cart-pulling (for large, powerful breeds such as mastiffs or rottweilers)

Of course, some of the exercises—and their length and level—depend on your dog's age, breed, and overall condition.

Encouraging your dog to drink plenty of water before, during, and after exercise ensures that she avoids dehydration and hyperthermia, conditions that can severely threaten health. On long extended walks, runs, or hikes, be sure to bring enough water along for both of you. If your dog is of medium size or larger, let her carry her own water bottles in a lightweight strap-on daypack made especially for dogs (available at most pet shops). The additional few added pounds taxes your dog's muscles a bit more, encouraging further strengthening and building endurance. Don't expect a smaller dog to carry her own water, as the added weight could hurt her back and overwork her body, and don't let big breeds drink large amounts of water in one sitting, as this behavior could lead to gastric bloat.

Grooming

A clean, well-cared-for dog stands a much better chance of living a longer, disease-free life than an unkempt, dirty animal. Dirt, bacteria, dead skin cells, loose hair, and air pollutants all collect on the surface of your dog's skin and hair. These discarded or unwanted materials produce an environment for the skin that predisposes it to bacterial infections, yeast infections, and parasitic infestations. These skin conditions can tax the animal's immune and antioxidant defense systems, reduce its reserves, thus setting the stage for the successful invasion of some other infectious disorder.

A filthy dog can suffer from various forms of dermatitis or skin disorders, ranging from red, inflamed areas or rashes to excess dandruff, eczema, or mange. Pores on the dog's skin become clogged with oily secretions, which serve as a food source for bacteria and yeast. All manner of parasites tend to infest the skin and coat of an unclean dog, including fleas, mites, ticks, and lice. When the stress of accumulated dirt, oils, and bacteria combines with the effects of parasites, the life of a chronically dirty dog can be cut short and made miserable.

A clean, well-groomed dog's system does not need to constantly contend with the stresses brought on by accumulated dirt, bacteria, pollutants, and parasites. Her skin and coat stay healthy, and she is happier due to less discomfort and stress. She won't have matted hair all over her body, an extremely uncomfortable condition when allowed to get out of hand. In addition, a dog who is used to being bathed, brushed, and combed actually grows to like the physical attention. Just think of how much we humans like to have our own hair brushed and our backs scratched!

BRUSHING AND COMBING

Consider thoroughly brushing your dog's coat at least 2 or 3 times each week, especially if yours is a longhaired breed such as a collie or Afghan. Choose a brush or a comb that best suits your dog's coat. Shorthaired dogs do well with a slicker-type brush, which has many small wire bristles designed to pick up loose hair, then easily come clean afterward. A dog with longer hair might do better with a more human-style metal comb.

With shorthaired breeds, lightly brush the dog's coat from head to toe, making sure to include her belly, tail, and legs. Avoid being too firm, but brush vigorously enough to stimulate the skin, which increases blood circulation to all areas. With longhaired breeds, separate a clump and begin combing the hair from its ends, slowly increasing the length, hence the depth, of hair combed. On a saluki, for instance, comb the first 3 to 4 inches of coat, then comb 1 inch closer to the skin and repeat, then closer again until you are finally combing the full length of the coat. This technique helps remove snarls and avoids the pain of a snagged brush. Take your time when combing a longhaired dog, remembering to clean hair from the comb frequently. As you do this, check the brush or comb for fleas. When you finish brushing and combing your dog, praise her lavishly, and give her a special healthy treat for a job well done. This teaches your pet that the brushing sessions are something to look forward to, not something to fear.

Bathing

Bathing, an essential part of grooming your dog, should be done when her coat becomes noticeably dirty and odorous, or if you detect parasites. Bathing can be a frequent occurrence or a rare one, depending of your dog's lifestyle and environment. An outdoor dog, for instance, needs more frequent bathing than a mellow little lapdog who spends most of her day curled up on a sofa. The general rule is: If she smells, bathe her! Avoid bathing her too often, though, as this can promote an overly dry skin and coat, and cause flaking or excess shedding—usually no more than once monthly.

Always comb your dog's hair before bathing her, making sure to remove all matted and snarled hair first. Bathing a dog with tangled or matted hair makes the tangles tighten up and become impossible to remove except with scissors, a technique that leaves empty spots in the dog's coat. Also before bathing, check the dog's body and feet for any foxtails, thorns, or other foreign objects, removing them before they cause discomfort. Then check for parasites, particularly fleas, which can be common during the warmer months and into late autumn. The presence of fleas or ticks may require the use of an herbal flea-and-tick dip and/or shampoo, an unnecessary measure when your pet is parasite-free. Consult your vet before selecting a flea-and-tick shampoo, as some off-the-shelf products can be ineffective and even toxic to your dog.

Next, determine where you want to bathe your dog. If it is a warm sunny day, you should have no problem doing it outside with the garden hose. If it is not warm out, or if you have a dog weighing under 20 or 25 pounds, you need a source of warm water to prevent your pet from becoming chilled. The bathtub works well for small dogs, provided you can attach some type of rubber hose to the spout, allowing you to thoroughly wet and rinse the dog. With a medium to large dog, you may want to consider finding a do-it-yourself "dogwash," or a groomer who lets you bathe your dog there for a nominal fee. These facilities have elevated tubs and warm running water, making the procedure easier for you to perform and more comfortable for your dog.

Choosing a shampoo depends on whether or not your dog has parasites or other skin diseases. If she doesn't, simply use a natural product that is pH-adjusted for dogs. Asking your vet for help in choosing the best shampoo ensures proper selection. Avoid using human shampoos, which are designed to support a human's pH level and not a dog's. Using the wrong shampoo can result in skin rashes, dandruff, or dry, brittle hair. (If your dog does have parasites, use a shampoo recommended by your vet—preferably one made from natural, nontoxic plant ingredients.)

Place your dog into the tub. Consider putting a rubber mat down first to minimize slipping and to give your pup a feeling of confidence. Gently and thoroughly wet her coat from her head to her rump with warm (not hot) water, working it into her fur as you go. As you do this, praise your dog, making her feel that the procedure is an enjoyable event. Then apply the shampoo, working it into her coat, building a good lather. Be careful not to get soap into your dog's eyes, ears, mouth, or nose, as this can be irritating and possibly painful. Massage the soap in completely, making sure to include the tail, belly, legs, neck, and head. If using a flea-and-tick shampoo (or nontoxic herbal shampoo), consider letting the suds sit on your dog's coat for 5 to 10 minutes, to allow the active ingredients time to kill or repel the parasites. Then thoroughly rinse her with warm water, taking care to remove all of the soap, which can cause irritation if left on. A particularly filthy dog may need a second wash and rinse. Otherwise, just towel-dry your dog as thoroughly as possible. If your dog will tolerate it, consider using a blow-dryer set on low heat, especially for longhaired breeds, whose coats can develop mildew if left damp.

Make sure you begin bathing your dog while she is still young. This desensitizes her to the procedure, making the job easier for you in future years. Even consider giving small, healthy food rewards before, during, and after the procedure to reinforce it as a positive experience.

NAIL TRIMMING

You need to periodically trim your dog's nails when they become too long, as excessively long nails can affect your dog's foot placement and create alignment problems with the toes, wrist, ankles, elbows, knees, shoulders, or hips. Nail trimming really needs to be started when your dog is young, as having her feet handled is rarely a happy experience for an adult dog. Starting early in your dog's life teaches her tolerance and shows her that she has nothing to fear.

Before even attempting to trim your dog's nails, you need to desensitize her to having her feet handled. For several days, while petting your dog, gently and casually handle each paw, massaging each between thumb and forefinger for a few seconds. Gradually make brief contact with each nail, then praise your dog for a job well done. After practicing this for a few days, begin lightly touching each nail with the clippers (available at any good pet shop) once or twice during the handling session. Avoid actually trimming yet; just get your dog used to the metallic feel of the clippers on her nails. Continue this procedure for a few more days, making sure to reward your dog with a treat, petting, and kind words after each session.

Once your dog has learned to tolerate having her feet and nails touched, try to very casually clip just one or two nails, making sure not to trim off more than 1/16 of 1 inch. At this point your goal is not to trim the nails as much as to desensitize the dog to the act, and to raise your own confidence and skill levels, important ingredients in successfully trimming your dog's nails. At this stage, be very conservative with your trimming; going too far will result in cutting into the "quick," a blood vessel running down the center of each nail. The nail's overgrown tip, usually no more than 1/8 to 1/4 of 1 inch long, is the only part with no quick in it. Cutting the quick causes the nail to bleed, and also creates a painful sensation that a dog does not soon forget. Also, cutting the nerve that runs just in front of the vessel could be quite painful, even if no bleeding occurs.

Once you and your dog are comfortable with trimming one or two nails, go ahead and do all of them, *remembering to trim only the very tips*. Be confident and fast, and be sure to praise your dog throughout the procedure. Make sure to have either a styptic pencil or powder or flour on hand; if you do happen to cut a quick and cause bleeding, gently packing the bleeding end with any of these neatly stops the flow of blood.

If the idea of trimming your dog's nails bothers or scares you, then don't do it. Let your groomer or vet do it instead. They are experienced at it and happy to do it for a fee.

EAR CLEANING

You should periodically inspect your dog's ears for dirt, parasites, wax buildup, or foreign debris, especially if she spends a great deal of time outdoors. Dirt and wax accumulations can lead to yeast and bacterial infections, which can affect hearing and balance and put undo stress on the immune system. A close visual exam should be followed by a check for any bad odor, which is often indicative of an infection.

To avoid these problems, clean your dog's ears at least once weekly by using an earwax solvent, almond oil, or diluted vinegar solution (one part vinegar to four parts water). Place 1 to 2 full eyedroppers of the chosen cleaning solution in the ear. Massage the outside of the ear canal to loosen the wax, enabling it to shake to the surface as soon as you let go of your dog and she shakes her head forcefully. Remove any dirt and wax that comes to the surface with cotton balls and cotton swabs. If you removed a lot of debris, repeat the process until no more debris can be seen, but do not clean deeper than you can see with the cotton swab. If the ear is inflamed, sore, odorous, abraded, or accumulating a lot more material than normal, see your vet. You also should see your vet if your dog frequently shakes her head or scratches and rubs her ears—even when no other symptoms are present.

After cleaning the ears, dry them with a clean, dry washcloth and/or cotton balls, then consider dusting each ear with a small amount of vet-approved ear powder to keep them dry and fresh-smelling. As with nail trimming, be sure to praise and reward your pet for putting up with the procedure, which she is likely to find tiresome at best.

Dental Hygiene

Sound dental care for your dog is an extremely important ingredient in maintaining and enhancing your dog's overall health; next to good nutrition, it may be the most important. The importance of this procedure does not lie in providing the dog with white teeth, a nice smile, and sweet breath. It lies in maintaining the health of the gums and reducing the bacteria and bacterial toxins in the mouth so that they do not become abundant enough to stress the liver and immune system. Most owners seriously neglect this area of hygiene, either because they do not realize its significance or do not know how to deal with the procedure.

Frequent inspection of your dog's teeth and gums, plus an annual dental cleaning by your vet, are as important for a dog as for a human being, perhaps even more so, for a number of reasons. First, a dog ages about seven times faster than a human being. Having her teeth examined and cleaned once per year equates to you having your teeth cleaned once every seven years! Would you ever go that long without a cleaning? Probably not. Taking your dog in for seven cleanings each year would be unreasonable and expensive—and require seven anesthetic procedures. A compromise is having your vet do an exam and cleaning once to twice yearly, depending on the condition of your dog's teeth and gums. Between cleanings, providing daily (or weekly, if that's more practical) oral hygiene is very important.

Tartar buildup on your dog's teeth becomes a rich source of food for bacteria, which multiply rapidly, convert the tartar to *plaque* and *calculus,* and release toxins into the dog's bloodstream. The bacteria and their toxins entering your dog's bloodstream can produce slow progressive diseases of the liver, kidney, heart, and lungs. Buildup of plaque and calculus eventually leads to periodontal disease, causing receding and bleeding gums as well as bone and tooth loss.

In order for your vet to perform a dental exam and cleaning, he or she needs to use a light general anesthetic. (An extremely safe gas anesthetic called Aerrane [isofurane] enables many dogs to be up and about 10 minutes after the procedure.) The use of this general anesthetic is necessary because most dogs do not passively submit to this invasive and stressful cleaning procedure. The *light* level of gas anesthesia used for dental work presents far fewer risks than the deeper levels required during surgical procedures, which allows it to be used on dogs who might normally be at too great a risk (due to advanced age or disease) for anesthesia use. Despite the relative safety of the procedure, a preanesthetic blood-screening and urinalysis will be done beforehand to detect hidden health problems. Intravenous fluid administration and the use of respiratory and oxygen monitors during a dental prophylaxis are often recommended for old or debilitated dogs.

At-Home Dental Care

In addition to the annual dental exam and cleaning by your vet, you should provide some form of daily dental hygiene. Brushing your dog's teeth daily would be great, but for most people it becomes too big a hassle and just doesn't get done. Therefore, I recommend rubbing an antibacterial gel (available through your vet) or colloidal silver (available at health-food stores) on your dog's gums once a day, supplemented by a weekly brushing.

When performing this weekly teeth cleaning, first open your dog's mouth and inspect its overall condition. Look for brown tartar buildup on the teeth (often found at or near the gumline), inflamed, bleeding, or excessively pale gums, or any sores, growths, or irritated areas. Any unusual observations you make should be noted in your medical log and reported to your vet for diagnosis and treatment. If you choose to use a canine toothpaste (some of which are meat-flavored, for more palatability), obtain one from your vet. You can use either a soft-bristled toothbrush or a relatively new item available in pet stores: a disposable, textured, finger-shaped implement that slips onto your own index finger, enabling you to brush your dog's teeth with your "fingertip."

The procedure is straightforward, and no different from the way you brush your own teeth. With your dog in a sitting position in front of you, open her mouth, lift a lip, and quickly brush the exposed teeth. Start with the fronts and move back methodically to each side, until you finish with the molars in back. Continue until all teeth top and bottom have been brushed. Take care to brush between teeth, as well massaging at the gumline.

Brushing half, or even a quadrant, of her teeth at a time, then taking time in between to play or rest may be easier, especially for adult dogs who don't have a long history of having their teeth brushed. After finishing each quadrant, praise your dog and give her a small treat. You can then continue on or rest for a few minutes, depending on how your dog is responding to the procedure. Remember to be positive and encouraging rather than severe and forceful. You don't want to teach your dog to dread the procedure.

Dog biscuits, dry food, and most chew toys do very little to help reduce tartar buildup. Keep in mind that we scrub our own teeth twice daily and still need semiannual cleanings: Do not be sold a bill of goods by manufacturers of these products. Also avoid giving your dog cooked bones, as over the years they can actually wear her teeth down, and may result in the perforation or obstruction of the intestinal tract. Raw bones, however, can be given instead.

Rawhide chews also should be avoided, as they can swell significantly in the stomach or intestines, causing life-threatening blockages. In addition, some rawhide chews may be treated with chemicals that can upset your pet's digestive tract. Cow hooves and pig ears, though not as threatening as rawhide, often contain growth hormones given to livestock to increase their body weight. These hormones can have a cumulatively bad effect on your dog's entire system.

Some of these measures may seem to be small details, but be assured that they play a large part in your pet's long-term health. They do require some effort and commitment, but they are very important to ensuring that your dog lives a long and healthy life.

Step 3. Create a Safe, Healthy Home Environment

Your dog spends the majority of his time in and around your home and yard. So it makes sense to keep this home environment as healthy, safe, and secure as possible to remove the threat of accidents, poisoning, attacks from other animals, or even escape. Nothing is more traumatic for an owner than discovering that his precious canine companion has gotten out of the yard or home and has been run over by a car, or has accidentally been poisoned by an open container of antifreeze, paint thinner, or garden chemicals.

Try to see things from a pet's view: What does your dog think, see, smell, and hear? What mischief is he most likely to get into? Remember that an adult dog has the reasoning capacity of a 2-year-old human, who is typically curious, mobile, and self-confident—with absolutely no concept of danger at all. Get down on your knees in your living room and look around. The view from this vantage point is just what your dog sees. Note that plants are right at eye level, as are cabinet drawers, coffee tables, television and stereo wiring, electrical outlets, power cords, and windowsills. This is your pup's point of view, so bear this in mind when attempting to dogproof all accessible areas.

Toxic Materials

All toxic materials should be removed from your pet's environment to prevent accidental poisoning and death. The most obvious substances—plants, cleaners, detergents, paint thinners, antifreeze, solvents, motor oil, and prescription drugs—must all be removed from your dog's world, as any one of them could quickly and painfully kill. Simply storing these substances behind a cupboard door is not enough, however, as some dogs learn how to open one with a deft flick of the paw. Of prime concern is the area below the kitchen sink, where many toxins are kept, along with the garbage, another potentially dangerous collection of substances. If you cannot move all of these items to an area outside of the reach of your dog, then install childproof locks on the doors to prevent a smart canine from getting to them.

Two other areas used to store toxic substances are the garage and basement. Yet many owners unwittingly put their dogs in these areas while they are away from home. If you looked in your garage or basement right now, you would probably find paint cans, antifreeze or motor oil, varied pesticides, grass fertilizer, paint thinner, loose nails, or spills of substances that could prove fatal if licked. If your dog has access to these areas, dogproof them by storing all toxic substances high up in the unreachable cupboards. Make sure the flooring is free from leaked motor oil, loose hardware, or anything else a curious pooch might innocently explore. (For a more complete list of toxic chemicals, see Appendix C, pp. 208–209.)

In addition to toxic chemicals, your dog could be poisoned by any number of common plants found in and around your home and garden. (See Appendix C, p. 208, for a list of toxic plants.) Be aware that plant toxins are often cumulative and may not produce outward toxic symptoms until a threshold level is reached. So do not assume a plant is safe for your dog to chew on just because the first few meals were uneventful. Outdoor decorative plants, such as azaleas or rhododendrons, are toxic to dogs if chewed regularly, as are parts of regular garden plants, including tomato- or bean-plant leaves and morning glory vines, and indoor houseplants, such as dieffenbachia or poinsettia. Cactus needles can be dangerous, particularly to your pet's eyes, mouth, and nose.

Dangerous Conditions

Hide or remove all electrical wires from your dog's usable area. A simple power cord, if plugged into a wall outlet, could be a death sentence to a teething puppy. Even low-voltage speaker wires can tangle around a playful dog's throat and possibly strangle him. Eating the wire itself can cause serious gastrointestinal damage, resulting in expensive surgery or death. Therefore, hide all wires underneath the carpeting, or at least run them along the edges of furniture or moldings, and secure them with heavy staples or duct tape. If you cannot hide these cords, then either keep them unplugged or spray them with a commercially available, bad-tasting substance. With dogs, out of sight is often out of mind.

Tall cabinets or bookshelves should be secured to the walls, using wire and one or two heavy-duty picture hangers, to prevent them from falling and possibly injuring a curious, playful pet. Make sure the bookshelves do not contain glass, sharp objects, or heavy items that could injure your pet if they topple. Christmas trees and decorations are also potential dangers during the holiday season.

A Doghouse

Whether placed in a backyard or inside the home, a doghouse of some sort, made either of wood or ready-made plastic (such as an airline travel crate) pleases most dogs. The doghouse is a private retreat for your pet, a place he can go to be alone, escape hectic activity, or just take a nap in peace. A place to call his own is a real comfort to your dog, and helps reduce stress. The aging dog in particular appreciates a safe, warm place to go, away from the hectic activity of children, puppies, or some other unpredictable activity.

Remember that dogs are territorial by nature, so giving yours an exclusive piece of territory (a den), albeit within your own, is good for his psychological well-being. Do not choose a doghouse made of wire, as this does not supply your dog with a sense of security or privacy. A wooden or plastic "house" with small wire openings on each side should be fine. Placing a washable blanket inside makes it comfortable and warm for your canine pal. (If you keep your dog outside during the winter months, the house should be insulated and a flap should be placed over the door to keep the wind out.)

The Yard

Your dog probably spends quite a bit of time in your yard, if you have one. Therefore make it a safe haven, not an accident waiting to happen. First, have a secure fence surrounding the yard to prevent escape that can lead to a lost or injured dog. It should be too high for your dog to jump over, bearing in mind that most dogs over 30 or 40 pounds can clear a four- to five-foot fence. A chain-link fence normally holds up better and costs less than a wooden fence, but a wooden fence provides more privacy and prevents your dog from seeing out of the yard and barking at passersby, a territorial behavior that may be reduced simply by removing the stimulus from sight. If you can afford the wooden fence, then go for it, as it is the better choice from a behavioral standpoint.

Most dogs are good diggers too, so make sure that the base of the fence is flush to the ground, with no open space whatsoever. The ground beneath the fence should be firm and turf-covered to discourage digging in the dirt. Make sure any holes or spaces large enough for your dog to get through are properly repaired to prevent escape and injury. For a dog particularly fond of digging, you may need to place concrete patio blocks along the fence to prevent any chance of escape.

Invisible fencing has been available to owners for some time now. This system uses wires buried beneath the yard's perimeter to produce mildly uncomfortable electrical stimulation that discourages your dog from stepping across a certain point. The stimulation occurs only to an animal wearing a special collar that receives signals from the perimeter wire. After a short training period, most dogs respond fairly well to the setup.

Invisible fencing does not work to keep other animals out of your yard, or to keep your dog in if it is sufficiently motivated to leave. A stray dog walking by, or even the paper carrier, could excite your dog enough for him to run right through the electrical barrier. Owners of highly territorial breeds such as rottweilers, mastiffs, Great Danes, or German shepherds may find this fencing ineffective.

Pools and Hot Tubs

If your home has a pool or outdoor hot tub, take care not to leave your dog in the yard unsupervised. Any size dog could fall into either source of water, get trapped, and eventually drown. The hot tub is lethal, particularly to small dogs, due to its high heat, which can dangerously lower blood pressure and produce hyperthermia. If you intend to keep your dog in a yard with a pool or hot tub, make sure it is securely covered or properly fenced when not in use. Even a covered pool can be dangerous if it accumulates a large pond of water on top of the cover, which can trap and drown a pet just like a pool would.

The Driveway and Street

Avoid allowing your dog to loiter in and around your driveway, as this highly trafficked area can be an accident waiting to happen. Often, visitors whip into your driveway without thinking that a dog might be lying on the warm asphalt, half-asleep in the morning or late afternoon sun. Older dogs are in particular jeopardy, as they cannot hear or see as well, and might not sense the presence of an oncoming car. Even if they see it coming, their older muscles and nervous systems might not work fast enough to get them to safety in time. Also, dogs allowed to stay around the driveway are more likely to run out into the street and get hit by a car. A nearby garage or driveway may also be dangerous if your neighbor has recently changed or replenished his or her antifreeze and left a puddle on the ground, which is quite attractive to dogs.

Try not to allow your dog to wander out into the road in front of your home, even in a quiet, rural setting, as this may allow an unfortunate, even fatal, accident (it is also most likely illegal in your area). At the very least, the habit of chasing cars or joggers may develop. Any dog allowed this level of freedom invariably begins to roam, which often leads to a lost, stolen, or injured animal. From the time your dog is a puppy, discourage roaming and independent access to the street. Even if your dog is older and already has this bad habit, it is not too late to modify. Keep him in a fenced backyard or indoors, taking him out only on a leash. Avoid playing catch or fetch near the street, as this could cause your dog to run out into the street after a treasured ball—into the path of a car. You wouldn't let your child play in the street, so show the same level of concern for your dog.

Other Domestic Animals

Other animals in and around your home can pose a substantial risk to your dog's health and well-being. A bite or scratch from a cat or dog can cause soft tissue wounds, infection, or broken bones, leading to profound psychological and physical stress.

Think carefully before adopting a second animal into your home.

If you are determined to do so, make sure that the new animal gets along with your resident dog. Ask if the owner, shelter, or breeder will allow you to bring your dog along to meet the "adoptee" on neutral territory. If the two animals get along, it will probably work out at home (though your older dog could become territorially aggressive on his home turf). Adopting adult cats can be risky, as they may not easily learn to tolerate dogs once they are beyond a few months of age. A cat scratch or bite is very infectious and can seriously affect your dog's health. A scratch to the eye could cause impairment of vision and lead to premature cataracts. Adopting a kitten with a puppy is a better option, as younger animals have less inclination to be aggressive or territorial (unless terrified).

Neighborhood dogs and cats who are allowed to roam freely can pose a threat to your dog's health, either from potential aggression or transmission of parasites or disease. These animals may enter your yard and find themselves under attack by your dog, who is acting out of normal territorial instincts. Even if no fighting or resultant injury ensued, these wayward pets may spread bacterial or viral infections, such as parvovirus, distemper, hepatitis, rabies, or give your pet a heavy infestation of fleas or worms. The older dog is especially prone to these invasions, as he has fewer immune-system reserves, and may no longer have the physical strength to deal with an aggressive stray animal as well as he once could.

To prevent stray domestic animals from entering your dog's territory, make sure to have a well-fenced yard. Do not feed strays and do not leave your dog's food dish outside overnight, particularly with food in it. Try to locate the owners of these free-roaming pets, and politely but firmly ask them to keep closer tabs on their pets. As a final step, report the stray animal to the local animal-control bureau, who will capture and hold the animal until the wayward owner picks him up and pays a fine to release the pet.

Wild Animals

Wild animals can pose a terrible threat to your dog. Raccoons, skunks, foxes, and bats have a very high incidence of rabies, a viral disease that will kill a dog who has not been vaccinated for it. Rats, in addition to carrying all manner of disease and parasites, can inflict serious bites when attacked. Raccoons, strong, clever creatures, certainly are more than a match for most dogs under 40 pounds. Coyotes, ever more common in Western rural and suburban areas, actually hunt down and kill dogs under 30 pounds, and can easily injure a larger dog. The older dog is particularly vulnerable to attack or infection from wild creatures, as his strength, agility, and senses are diminished. Despite this danger, the older pet often acts more upset and aggressive toward wild invaders due to a lifetime of territorial habits.

Avoid the intrusion of wild animals into your dog's territory by keeping no food of any type in the area, including leftover dog food in a dish, bags of birdseed, open garbage containers, or unharvested fruits or vegetables. Keep your grass cut and clear out high weeds and overgrown patches of ivy and thick brush, which make great cover for rodents. Check your roof and attic for rat, mice, or raccoon nests or droppings, and call your exterminator if you find any signs of infestation. If any poison is used by the exterminator, make absolutely sure that your dog cannot get anywhere near it, and make sure that, after the vermin are eradicated, you remove all toxic materials. Do not approach a nest of baby rats, raccoons, or skunks, as the parents can be quite vicious in defense. Instead, call animal control to deal with it.

Most important, make sure your dog has had a rabies vaccination, which needs to be augmented every three years (or sooner, depending on age) by law. Proper precautionary measures could help save or lengthen your pet's life, so innoculate, and clear out those unwanted animals from your dog's territory.

Snakes and Toads

A bite from a poisonous snake or reptile can be fatal to your dog. Certain areas of the country, particularly the Southeast and Southwest, have a resident population of poisonous reptiles with which your dog could come into contact. A good number of curious canines do, in fact, succumb to bites from rattlesnakes or water moccasins each year. These unfortunate events usually occur on hiking trips, when the dog gets far out ahead of his owner. Coming into contact with a dangerous creature, the dog goes over to investigate, usually with a quick sniff. A bite from a mature rattlesnake, unless treated immediately, kills a dog under 60 pounds and either kills or seriously sickens larger canines. Another possible threat comes from poisonous toads. If your pet likes to chase and bite these wild animals, he could unknowingly poison himself.

To avoid such unfortunate situations, make sure that you know just what types of wildlife commonly inhabit an area where you and your dog go walking or hiking. If you suspect that poisonous reptiles might be present, consider keeping your dog on a leash to prevent him from getting out of sight and into trouble. For the times that your dog is off-leash, make sure to teach him a reliable "come" command. If you see your pet headed into harm's way, a command to "come" could save his life. Teaching your dog to "leave it" is another useful command that simply requires the dog to leave alone anything he is investigating. In order to have your dog reliably respond to commands, he needs obedience training. Taking a class and reading as many training books as possible should help you achieve this goal, provided you have patience and leadership abilities.

Poisonous Spiders and Insects

Some insect bites can be toxic to your dog. Certain spiders, ants, bees, wasps, and hornets can inflict serious bites, some of which, particularly those from black widow spiders, can be fatal. Multiple bee, wasp, or hornet stings also may be fatal, especially to smaller dogs. Again, be sure to educate yourself regarding which poisonous insects are in your area, and discuss with your vet steps you should take if your pet is bitten. Make sure to rid your dog's territory of hives and nests containing poisonous bees, wasps, hornets, or ants. If necessary, call a professional exterminator to help you. Remove stingers as quickly as possible from an injured dog and treat the affected area with ice or cool cloths *while on the way to your vet.*

Disappearing Dogs

Nothing is as heart-wrenching as losing a beloved dog, whether he runs away or is stolen. Dogs often run away after a move to a new home in a different neighborhood, when any dog is upset by the sudden disappearance of his familiar territory—to the degree that he may try to leave and seek it out. Dogs taken on vacations also may become stressed and confused, often resulting in their running away. Sometimes leaving the gate to the fence open results in a curious dog casually straying from his yard. Some breeds are particularly prone to wandering when given the opportunity. Arctic breeds, such as malamutes, huskies, and Samoyeds, as well as sighthounds such as salukis, Afghans, whippets or greyhounds, are wanderers at heart, but they should not be allowed to cruise the neighborhood.

Losing your dog, especially in an area unknown to you and your pet, can result in death for your beloved companion, either by being hit by a car or by being euthanized by animal-control officers who routinely destroy recovered dogs not claimed after a limited time period (often as short as 3 days). The simple stress of being lost and separated from his pack—your family—can affect the health of a dog, particularly an older animal who, after being in a familiar environment for many years, suddenly finds himself lost and, from his viewpoint, abandoned. The older dog also has less ability to stay out of trouble due to his diminished strength and speed. He may not be able to get out of the way of a car fast enough or defend himself against other animals well enough.

As a dog owner, your responsibility is to avoid letting this happen. First, make sure that all fences and gates are secure and high enough to prevent your dog from escaping. If you have a terrier, breeds known for their digging skills, make sure your fence goes right down to the turf—not bare dirt, which is an open invitation for digging. If your dog tends to be a digger, consider mounting the bottom of the fence into a concrete border, or placing concrete patio blocks along the border of the fence line.

Take care not to leave front or back doors to your home open, as your dog's natural curiosity draws him outside. If you have children, make sure they understand the importance of keeping the doors closed. Leaving car windows rolled down too far also allows for a lost dog. If, when running into the store on warm summer days, you want to crank down the windows a bit lower than normal to prevent your pet from overheating, purchase a wire grill device (available at most pet shops) that easily fits into the window track of your car. This allows plenty of ventilation, while preventing the dog from squeezing through the window and suddenly finding himself alone in a strange neighborhood. However, never leave your dog in a hot car for more than 5 or 10 minutes, even with the windows open.

When planning a trip, consider leaving your pet at home. Either ask a reliable neighbor to take care of him or hire a dog-sitter to visit 2 or 3 times a day. A dog prefers the familiarity of his own territory; leaving him home alone for a week or so may be less stressful than taking him with you, even though he misses you. Certain breeds, however, may develop severe separation anxiety when away from you. German shepherds, Doberman pinschers, and dalmatians are especially prone to this, so consider taking them with you. If you must take your dog on a trip, always keep him on a leash to prevent him from running away in a strange territory.

Leaving your dog with a family member, neighbor, or person who boards animals in their house can be a precarious situation. A dog kept in strange surroundings prefers to get back to his own house and therefore may look for opportunities to escape. He may easily jump or crawl under or through a hole in your friend's fence, or bolt out as children open the gate or front door. The people with whom you left your dog may not realize this danger, or take the necessary precautions to prevent escape, so explain to them all the precautions you follow regarding the yard and outdoor walks.

A well-trained dog is much less likely to become lost. Often, a dog runs away from his owner while being exercised off-leash at parks simply because the owner has not taught him a reliable "come" or "stay" command. A poorly trained animal who sees another dog down the block may just take off after her, despite his owner's pleadings. The solution is a simple one: Train your dog! Attend obedience classes before ever taking your dog's leash off outside. Also, consider purchasing a leash that extends to over 30 feet in length, which allows your dog a good amount of freedom while preventing him from running away.

The single most important step for ensuring that you can recover a lost dog is to make sure he is wearing a proper identification tag, license, and rabies vaccination tag on a secure collar. A tag with your name and telephone number on it (along with your veterinarian's phone number) very often makes a huge difference. Without any form of identification, a well-meaning person who finds your pet has no way of finding you. Your dog may end up in a shelter, which might eventually euthanize your pet. Some owners have their vets painlessly inject a small microchip just under the skin into the dog's neck folds. This device, which can be scanned at most shelters or vet clinics, provides all the necessary information for finding you (providing you have paid a lifetime registry fee). Your vet can even tattoo your dog with all the vital information, usually placing the tattoo on the belly, ear, or inner thigh where there is little hair. A collar with a metal or plastic ID tag containing an address or phone

number should be worn by all dogs—even if your dog has been tat-
tooed or injected with a microchip.

If, despite all precautions, your dog becomes lost, do not panic—
often the dog is found. Call and visit all local animal shelters in your
vicinity as often as possible, making sure that you have filed a
missing-dog report with each. With the help of some friends with
cars, thoroughly canvass your area to about a square mile or so (or
farther, if you have an arctic breed or sighthound). Look in yards,
parks, and around garbage containers. While doing so, post as many
lost-dog notices as possible. Include all pertinent descriptive information, such as color, size, gender, age, eye color, and name. Include a photo and the date and location he was lost—and be sure to
list your telephone number.

Offering a reward sometimes motivates people who might not
otherwise help, so consider doing so. Also, place a lost-dog ad in the
local paper and telephone all the vet clinics and police stations in
the area, on the chance that your injured dog was brought in by
some good samaritan. Last, speak to all of the children in the area,
as well as mail and paper carriers, who all have an intimate feel for
the goings on in the neighborhood. Above all, do not give up, and
keep checking in with the shelters and police.

By creating a safer, more pet-friendly environment for your dog,
you will dramatically reduce the odds that something unexpected
and injurious will occur. Feeding your dog the best food in the world
won't mean a thing if she gets hit by a car, hurt by another animal,
poisoned, or hopelessly lost. Remember, part of extending your
dog's life involves preventing accidental mishaps, which can age a
pet dramatically. A three-year-old dog who has her hips smashed by
a car will suddenly be similar to a fifteen-year-old with arthritis.
Both dogs will be unable to exercise, and neither will be very happy.
In review, make sure to:

- Eliminate all potentially toxic substances in and around your
  home.

- "Dog-proof" your home and property.
- Safeguard your dog against potentially dangerous animals and insects.
- Take all necessary steps to prevent car accidents.
- Train your dog in order to better prevent her from running away.
- Supervise her closely.

Step 4. Avoid Behavioral Problems

Unacceptable behavior is the most common cause of people giving up their pets or sacrificing them to early euthanasia. An obedient pet is a joy and contribution to the family. Obedience makes the human-animal bond strong and motivates the pet's owner to provide the best care available in order to continue this loving relationship as long as possible. If a dog is disobedient, dangerous, and destructive, the owner finds little reason to go out of his way to maintain the health of his pet.

All animals need to learn in order to survive. The wild animal who learns to find food, socialize, procreate, and avoid danger will have the best chance of living a long, healthy life. The dog, once a wild animal, is now considered a domesticated creature; his form, function, and environment are all determined by human beings. Nevertheless, domestic canines still have the same basic instinct as wild wolves. They strive to belong to a socially stratified pack, protect their territories, and remain predatory. People have spent so much time close to our canine companions over the centuries, though, that we tend to think of them only in human terms. In fact, the human and dog species are quite similar. Both are highly social, with complex emotional ties to a group; both share a history of territorial, hunting behavior; and both are devoted to rearing their young, using complex systems of communication.

Where the human species differs, however, is in our evolution toward relatively democratic methods of government, compared to the canine autocratic system. Dogs identify the leader of their pack, then gladly obey that leader. Each dog finds his place in the pack hierarchy; the dog at the bottom knows to submit to all the others, whereas the leader knows that he has dominance over all of the pack. This rigid pack loyalty has helped dogs prosper, ensuring their survival through reliance on complex, militaristic hunting regimes.

An owner who does not become a responsible leader to her dog does her a great disservice. Your dog needs leadership to feel safe, confident, and comfortable. If you don't assume the role of leader, you force your dog to take on the role herself—even if she's not capable of fulfilling it. An owner who spoils a dog and makes her the center of attention, giving her whatever she desires without making her earn it, mistakenly shows the dog that she is the leader. When a dog thinks she is the leader, several things occur. First, she feels the added pressure of having to lead her "pack." Second, she assumes that she has the right and responsibility to discipline and control the "lesser" members of the pack, including you, your spouse, your children, and anyone else who comes into the territory.

When a dog has not received some type of obedience training, she gradually assumes a cavalier, dominant attitude and becomes difficult to control, which jeopardizes her physical and psychological health. An untrained dog often gets into fights with other dogs who she thinks are "invading" her territory, a behavior that can result in injury. Dogs with little or no training also tend to run away, or at the very least disregard the command "come," which can lead to a lost dog, injury or death from an automobile, or euthanasia by animal-control officers. Untrained dogs who assume the mantle of leadership may even become aggressive toward humans—a sure path to euthanasia.

The stress caused by a lack of leadership and structure in a dog's life can lead to a physical illness. Eating and elimination problems, as well as behavioral disorders, can appear when a dog has no one to look to for guidance. An unruly dog also is no fun to be with, which could lead to being given away for adoption, with doubtful prospects at best.

Obedience training also provides your dog with something on which to focus. Remember that all dog breeds were originally designed with a particular duty in mind, whether herding, guarding, retrieving, or something else. Owners who do not give their dogs a "job" to do run the risk of their pets becoming bored, anxious, stressed, and destructive. Obedience training gives your dog something to think about and achieve, helping her learn to think rather than simply react to stimuli in a mindless fashion. Teaching tricks or fun exercises, such as fetch or catch, can focus your dog's attention and get her to look forward to learning—always a healthy mind-set.

Basic Training for Dogs up to 2 Years of Age

Even before you acquire a new puppy, be sure to get—and read—a basic obedience-training manual to get a general feel for technique, expectations, supplies, and recommendations. In addition, reading a book on basic canine psychology helps improve your ability to communicate with and empathize with your dog. Most basic-training manuals are similar in methodology, so choose one that you feel most comfortable with in terms of style and clarity. Avoid any books that suggest using overly harsh training methods, such as striking or yelling at the dog, as these are ineffective and only serve to create stress, resulting in undesirable behavior or illness.

Training can begin when the dog is 8 to 10 weeks old; however, it is advised to wait until the puppy is 12 weeks old since the period between 8 and 11 weeks of age is known as the fear-imprint stage. If anything traumatic happens during this 3-week span, it can affect the dog's behavior for the rest of her life. During this short period, also avoid unpredictable environments or places with loud noises or sudden occurrences. Fireworks, hectic urban settings, or any loud venues should be off-limits until the puppy is a full 3 to 4 months of age.

The beginning stages of training should involve rudimentary behaviors, including proper housebreaking, walking on a loose leash, general manners, and basic commands such as "sit," "down," "stay," and "come." General rules of behavior should be established for the young dog, so that she knows what you, the leader, expect from her. Strongly discourage basic no-no's, such as mouthing your hands, jumping, begging, growling, or excessive barking, as soon as possible, so that the puppy does not internalize the behaviors and carry them with her for a lifetime. Changing these behaviors is much harder to do with an older dog who has had years to grow accustomed to them. Working on getting them right from the first day makes the rest of your lives together much easier. An older dog can, of course, learn new or better behaviors, but that takes more time and patience on your part.

Whatever training methods you decide to use, following these few basic guidelines ensures a well-trained, happy dog:

1. Establish yourself as a leader, not a sibling, so that your dog is motivated to learn and please, not to compete. Establish yourself at the top of the pack to improve obedience and reduce or prevent aggression.
2. Use positive, reward, and praise-based methods of teaching, and avoid at all times the use of yelling or hitting, which only serve to frighten the dog and create a plethora of new, undesirable behaviors.
3. Supervise the young, untrained animal as much as possible for at least the first year of her life. A young dog allowed to wander the home or neighborhood without guidance learns atrocious habits and becomes her own leader, causing behavioral problems.
4. Praise good behavior and correct bad behavior as soon as they occur, not after the fact. Your dog lives in the moment; if you

punish her for eliminating on the carpet, do so when the mistake occurs or immediately after (within 15 to 30 seconds), and not 4 or 6 hours in the future. An owner who comes home hours after the undesirable event has happened and punishes the dog merely confuses her, and in turn, the dog learns that the arrival of her master is a time to hide. She has no idea that the punishment is for something that happened hours ago.

5. Vary the behaviors taught to your dog. Rather than just teaching the basic behaviors, include some that are fun and exciting for both of you. Trick training is a great way to expand your dog's intellect while having fun and bonding more closely.

6. Keep each training session as brief and focused as possible. Once you see improvement on one specific task, stop the session and praise your pup lavishly.

Obedience Classes

Dogs of all ages can benefit from attending a basic obedience class once a week, for seven to ten weeks, usually. Whether held at a local or county shelter, or a private institution, classes led by a professional dog trainer can make a world of difference in your dog's behavior. In addition to having a professional guide you through a structured, proven course of study, you have the added benefit of working your dog in front of numerous other owners and dogs. This advantage is twofold: First, you are able to gauge your dog's performance (and your own) in comparison to the others; second, your dog can socialize with other humans and dogs, an important key to creating a healthy, calm mind-set for your pet.

Ideally, take your dog to obedience classes as early on as possible. Puppies from 12 weeks of age and up can benefit immensely from this early contact with structured learning. Adult dogs also benefit, albeit more slowly. Realize that social habits developed over many years are hard to modify in an older dog. A 10-year-old, highly territorial German shepherd, for instance, is not likely to become a social butterfly overnight. In fact, the instructor may ask the owners of older, potentially aggressive dogs to guard against their pets coming too close to other dogs or persons in the class (basically for liability reasons). This should not dissuade you from attempting to teach your old curmudgeon of a dog "new tricks." Just being in a new learning environment is often a positive step toward eliminating bad behaviors and the stress they can cause.

Working with the Older Dog at Home

The older dog can benefit from regular training sessions with you at home, whether to fine-tune existing behaviors or learn entirely new ones, such as a trick or two. Keeping your older dog's mind alert and working helps maintain her mental acuity and gives her something to look forward to, rather than just lying around waiting for her next meal. All dogs, young or old, need to feel as if they have some purpose in life. Without a purpose or something to look forward to, dogs, like humans, become restless, anxious, and apathetic.

Consider teaching your dog to become attached to one specific toy, perhaps a ball or a stuffed animal. In doing so, you give yourself a unique tool that both motivates and rewards proper behavior. Working canines, such as bomb-sniffing or search-and-rescue dogs, are trained to know that when they perform properly, they are rewarded with their favorite toys. Often the attachment to a particular toy is even stronger than the desire to receive a food reward, which avoids allowing your pet to become overweight from too many treats.

Be more patient when teaching an older dog any new behavior, since she won't learn as fast as that 12-week-old puppy. Also, avoid teaching the elderly dog any strenuous or athletic new behaviors; her advanced years may no longer provide her with the endurance, coordination or strength needed to perform. Older bones, muscles, ligaments, and tendons do not respond well to jumping and running;

instead choose less active tricks or behaviors. Rather than teaching her to jump over a five-foot fence, train her to balance a cookie on her muzzle or seek out and find a hidden cookie by using her sense of smell. Use common sense, avoiding behaviors that could injure the animal and thereby lessen her quality of life.

The older dog may begin to forget how to perform certain behaviors or tricks if they are not reinforced at regular intervals, so practice established basic obedience or tricks at least 1 time a week with the older animal. Go over the basic commands ("sit," "down," "come," and "stay"), then work whatever tricks she knows and loves.

Advancing Age and Its Effects on Behavior

Your dog's behavior can and will be affected by the constraints of advancing age. The older dog, no longer as spry, agile, or strong as she once was, slowly loses the ability to perform athletic feats that were once second nature to her. Running for extended periods of time, jumping over high objects, making sharp turns, or even enjoying horseplay with you or other dogs becomes more difficult or even impossible for the aging animal, whose body just won't perform up to previous standards any longer.

As your dog ages, her muscle mass is reduced at the same time that her overall body weight increases. The loss in "horsepower" combined with the gain in weight translates into a slower response time and loss of strength. In addition, her skeletal system becomes weaker and more brittle, her heart and lungs less efficient, and her nervous system less responsive. All of these combine to slow the dog down and make her more vulnerable to injury, which can, in turn, further advance aging.

The limitations of advancing age also affect your dog's moods and overall temperament. A normally happy, outgoing animal who begins to suffer from old-age "slow down" can sometimes become stressed, confused, and irritable. For instance, a 12-year-old Labrador retriever used to fetching a tennis ball for hours on end may become perplexed and sullen when an encroaching arthritic condition curbs her once-youthful zeal, slowing her down or causing her pain. The same may happen to the older dog who has gained weight and lost muscle mass; she just can't seem to understand why she isn't performing up to her old standards anymore.

In addition to becoming depressed or anxious, many dogs facing their limitations sometimes display new, undesirable behaviors ranging from breaking housetraining to outright disobedience or aggression. The older dog who experiences sudden pain while performing a familiar and enjoyable behavior may become irritable to the point of displacing her anger onto others around her. In other words, when in pain a normally sweet-tempered dog can become an unhappy, intolerant animal, capable of growling or biting.

The slowing down or failure of various organ systems in your dog's body can also cause undesirable behavioral and physical changes. A less efficient cardiovascular system, for instance, causes a gradual reduction in the supply of blood to all areas of the body and, hence, a degeneration of all the organ systems. Over the years, reduced blood supply to the brain can cause the gradual onset of senility, leading to an overall breakdown in behavior. The internal organs all function less efficiently, possibly affecting appetite and elimination habits. With advancing age, your pet could suffer problems with incontinence due to a failing urinary-tract system and a loss of tone or atrophy of the sphincter muscles.

Decreasing neural response slows down your dog's reaction time, causing a delay when obeying commands. The aging dog's sense of hearing is diminished with time, also causing her to respond more slowly, which may increase the threats to her well-being. The near-deaf dog, for instance, may not hear a car coming or your frantic commands to "come." Failing vision has a similar effect on your dog's behavior, perhaps to an even greater degree. She won't see a car or an aggressive dog coming toward her, and won't see the thorny rosebush or the edge of the deck she is walking toward. Curiously, the aging dog's sense of smell is rarely diminished over time; geriatric dogs rely on it more and more.

Other undesirable behaviors can appear as your dog ages. Excessive barking may become a problem when a dog begins to experience the physical discomforts of aging, as can other problems such as digging, stealing possessions, or general destructiveness. An irritable, aging dog, in response to the confusion of old-age "slow-down," might release her stress by tearing up a sofa, destroying a carpet, or chewing your favorite pair of boots, behaviors that haven't been prevalent since puppyhood.

All dogs become very attached to the routine of their lives. By the time your dog is 8 to 10 years old, her day-in and day-out traditional routine are extremely comforting. The predictability of the morning walk, the evening feeding, the weekend swim, or the daily playtime is a great comfort. So any profound change in the older dog's routine, whether due to new medical limitations or a sudden change such as a move, the death of another animal in the home, or the sudden departure of one or more family members from the "pack," can significantly affect her behavior for the worse and produce psychological stress, which wears heavily on the immune and antioxidant-defense systems. Abrupt changes can cause a breakdown in housetraining, as well as destructive behavior, depression, disobedience, or loss of appetite. They can even result in the dog running away and being injured or killed.

Minimizing the Effects of Age on Behavior

You can take various steps to prevent or minimize undesirable behavior in the aging dog. First and foremost, ensure that your pet is receiving the best nutrition possible to help minimize old-age "slow down." (See Step 5, pp. 100–126, for further information on nutrition.) Also avoid instituting abrupt changes in your dog's diet and routine, as these can cause stress and erratic behavioral problems. Keep her life as routine as possible to guarantee stability and predictability. Any necessary changes should be instituted very slowly, over several weeks of time.

As the caring owner of an older dog, you need to reevaluate her environment and perhaps gradually make it less taxing or dangerous. A dog who once was accustomed to jumping up into the back of a pickup truck, for instance, needs to be taught a new method of entry as she ages, to prevent strains, sprains, tears, or unnecessary injury to her hips, back, or shoulders. Providing a dog with a ramp, lifting her into the bed, or allowing her to ride in the cab with you are all viable alternatives.

An older dog living outside in a cold, inclement environment may need to be reconditioned slowly into living indoors in the home or garage, due to the deleterious effects that severe weather can have on her body. Likewise, a dog who is used to performing at a high athletic level gradually needs to find less-taxing activities to enjoy. A 2-year-old Newfoundland who enjoys swimming for 3 hours each morning will not be capable of the same level of activity when she reaches 8 or 10 years of age. Shorter, more frequent swims put less stress on this giant breed's cardiovascular system, often the Achilles' heel of this friendly dog's body.

Making the aged dog as comfortable as possible helps relieve pain and helps prevent erratic behavior. Providing the pet with a soft blanket or bed to sleep on relieves pressure on achy joints and gives added insulation from the cold, hard floor or ground, a godsend for dogs with advanced arthritis. Keeping the home warm and dry also lessens the effects of arthritis and helps keep older, stiffer muscles and joints more limber. Because the older dog may be suffering from a loss of hearing and/or vision, take care not to surprise her while she sleeps, as this can be startling and frightening to her. Some dogs may react defensively to this sudden intrusion and could bite as an instinctive defense. Either let her awaken on her own or lightly slap the floor a few yards away, which sends vibrations that should awaken her.

If your dog begins to have trouble hearing, consider training her to respond to hand signals rather than just audible commands. You can develop your own type of sign language that the dog readily responds to, as all canines are very conscious of body postures and movements. The opposite is true for an older dog with failing vision: Make sure to use spoken commands rather than hand signals. Also ensure that the dog's environment is as clutter-free as possible to prevent her from bumping into things and hurting herself. In general, be more observant of the dog with failing vision or hearing, as she could get into trouble without realizing it.

Although the aging dog should not be expected to perform any physically taxing tricks or behaviors, she should be kept active throughout her remaining years. Take her for frequent walks to keep her bones, joints, and muscles in good shape and to provide her with adequate stimulation. Replace running with walking, or jumping with finding a hidden treat. Massage the elderly dog 1 time daily to maintain circulation and soothe achy muscles and joints.

The aging dog who is kept healthy exhibits fewer behavioral problems than the pet who harbors an undiagnosed illness. Consider taking the older dog to the veterinarian for semiannual, rather than annual, checkups to ensure better health. It gives your vet a chance to catch a medical problem before it gets out of hand. Have blood, urine, and stool samples taken for analysis. Also, pay more attention to the older dog's teeth, which may begin to show signs of wear or decay, and have your vet check her gums and teeth for gingivitis and periodontal disease at the semiannual visit.

The aging canine needs more attention paid to the condition of her skin, coat, nails, and ears. As a dog ages, her coat and skin can dry out; she can develop skin allergies, alopecia (hair loss), "hot spots" (sensitive, itchy areas that she incessantly chews on, leaving red and raw spots), nail fungi, and ear infections. Increasingly frequent grooming sessions help deal with these problems and prevent any behavioral problems that they might generate.

The Importance of Social Interaction

Most dogs crave companionship of some sort, largely due to their canine "pack" instinct. Belonging to and working with a group is second nature to all dogs, and is essential to maintaining good mental health. Dogs learn from the group and generally thrive in social, interactive surroundings. Because your dog sees you and your family as pack members who are above her in the hierarchy, you become her role models and she is never happier than when surrounded by you.

A dog who is isolated from contact with humans or other animals becomes unhappy, depressed, stressed, and perhaps even destructive. Unlike cats, dogs must have regular doses of companionship in order to stay mentally alert and at ease. A dog who hardly ever interacts with others eventually suffers from a variety of behavioral and physical disorders, including incessant barking, digging, scratching, crying, pacing, sleep disorders, loss of appetite, skin rashes, infections of various types, destructive behavior, and hair loss, to name a few. The isolated, deprived dog is more likely to run away, or even bite, out of frustration or anger. Her immune system, drained by the emotional trauma or stress of being alone, is not able to fight off disease, which allows her to succumb to bacteria, viruses, fungi, and parasites.

From early on in life, allow your dog to interact with as many people and animals as possible. Sadly, many owners do not allow this to happen for various reasons, whether falling into a rut by always staying close to home or fearing that their dogs are borderline aggressive in some manner and thereby never taking them out in public. Overall, many dogs end up living the lives of hermits and become increasingly suspicious and distrustful of others.

From the time your dog is a puppy, make sure you spend ample time training, exercising, and simply interacting with her. Try to get your dog out and away from your home as much as possible, taking walks down active, residential streets. Introduce her to neighbors and their pets and allow her to see and hear the sounds of the world around her. Bring small, healthy treats with you and allow others to give them to your dog; this teaches her that other persons are not to be feared. (Don't worry: a well-socialized dog still defends your home from burglars!) Encourage paper and mail carriers to bond with your dog to avoid later problems. Take your dog to enclosed, regulated off-leash parks or get some of the neighbors and their dogs together to enable socialization. Doing so on a regular basis also minimizes the chances of dogfights on your block. Your dog's confidence level can soar, putting her at ease with strangers and creating a healthier emotional state of mind.

If your dog is extremely antisocial and afraid of strangers, don't force her to go out among the public to be petted, which is unfair on your part. Shy, timid dogs can be taken for walks on a leash, within sight of social activity, without having to make actual contact. This is a good way to gradually ease the fearful or aggressive dog back into the real world. In conjunction with this, working with a professional canine behaviorist can help tremendously in solving deeply rooted antisocial tendencies in your dog.

Take time out each day to be with your dog. Work on some new tricks. Play ball. Get down on the floor and give each other a hug. Make lots of physical contact, and include petting, massaging, and soft talking. These social interactions are cherished by your dog, whose health and well-being are greatly enhanced by the experience.

Young dogs aren't the only ones who need socialization. Older dogs need just as much, particularly with you, the "leader." They need to feel that their advancing age doesn't mean they are any less important to the "pack." The older dog may have less patience with small children who want to play roughly or with other dogs, as she isn't as capable of "defending" herself or getting away from an unpleasant situation. To avoid an irritable dog or an unpleasant situation, simply talk to the children beforehand, asking them to be respectful and gentle. Let them give the older dog some treats, to allay her concerns. When introducing your older dog to a young, frisky dog, do so gradually, ideally for short periods of time and away from your home, so that your dog does not feel a territorial violation. Make sure to reward your dog with healthy treats during and after the meeting. Keeping your dogs socially active and aware of the world around her is one key to keeping her happy and healthy. Another, proper nutrition, is covered in the next step.

Step 5. Optimize Nutrition

Providing your dog with the right food and nutritional supplements, when fed in the proper amounts, helps prevent disease and degeneration and substantially retards the aging process. If a genetically sound dog is fed a food free of toxins, comprised of a wide variety of fresh whole ingredients, and properly formulated and balanced with regard to age, breed, environment, and lifestyle, that dog is better equipped to handle stress, resist disease, and maintain himself in the best health possible. Before applying the principles of good nutrition, you need to first understand them.

The True Value of Food

What your dog takes into his body as food plays a major role in determining how his body copes with disease and the ravages of aging. The food you feed your pet can either strengthen him by providing building blocks for a healthy, disease-resistant body or injure him by introducing toxic substances to his various canine tissues and organ systems. The single most effective way for you to extend the life of your dog is to choose a diet that provides him with all the essential nutrients in fresh, optimal amounts and in the most digestible and absorbable forms, while simultaneously eliminating any toxins in his diet.

A host of potentially toxic substances can be introduced into your dog's diet without you even knowing. These could be the chemicals sprayed on crops as they grow, or those fed to livestock to promote their growth. Pesticides, herbicides, antibiotics, and hormones, all routinely used by farmers and ranchers to maximize growth and profits, weaken your dog's body, clearing a pathway for disease and degeneration. Other chemicals added during manufacturing, such as preservatives, taste enhancers, coloring agents, and emulsifiers, may also have degenerative effects on your dog's health.

Nutritional deficiencies, excesses, imbalances, and toxins can have an impact on your dog's body in ways that tend to weaken his digestive and immune systems. The liver and kidneys, responsible for detoxification, may become overtaxed. The dog's glandular regulatory system also is often affected (frequently by added hormones found in meat and meat by-products). In general, nutritional deficiencies and toxins reduce the innate healing powers of the canine body, and open up the way for degeneration and premature aging.

Too much of a good thing also can injure your dog's health. If a food contains too much fat or an overabundance or imbalance of certain vitamins or minerals, for instance, your pet's metabolism could be adversely affected, as could the function of the various organ systems. Some nutrients that ordinarily have beneficial effects for one dog could act as an allergen for another, producing reactions toxic to the canine body. Many dogs can and do develop allergies to common ingredients, such as wheat, soy, corn, and even beef, and require alternative sources of nutrition.

Sadly, over the past fifty years, foods consumed by both humans and dogs have deteriorated in nutritional value, while becoming increasingly toxic. Farm-fresh meats, grains, vegetables, and fruits, once grown under less polluted conditions, are now tainted by all manner of chemicals, preservatives, additives, bleaches, and nutrient-draining processing. Overrefined, laden with saturated fats, salt, and sugar, and deficient in whole grains, complex carbohydrates, and fresh meat, many dog foods are becoming increasingly deficient in the vitamins, minerals, essential fatty acids, phytochemicals, beneficial bacteria, and enzymes needed to sustain good health. Consider the following nutrients and how each contributes to creating a healthy body.

Nutrients: Essential and Nonessential

Your dog's body needs food to function. Some important nutrients can be manufactured by the body and are therefore considered nonessential. Other required nutrients cannot be synthesized by your dog's body, and so must be consumed in the foods he eats. Such nutrients are known as essential nutrients.

PROTEIN: ESSENTIAL AMINO ACIDS

The main structural component of tissues and organs, your dog needs protein to grow and repair cells and form antibodies and enzymes. Protein is composed of individual units called *amino acids*; some are manufactured within the body and others can only be obtained from a proper diet. Protein in your dog's diet can come from either animal or plant sources. Some breeds, particularly those who are more active (such as hunting dogs), may have a higher requirement for protein than other breeds. The ten essential amino acids that your dog needs are *arginine, histidine, isoleucine, leucine, lysine, methionine, phenylalanine, threonine, tryptophan,* and *valine.*

CARBOHYDRATES

The main energy source for the body, carbohydrates are required for metabolism to take place. Coming mostly from plant materials, the basic types of carbohydrates are simple and complex sugars. In order for your dog to fully digest and metabolize plant carbohydrates, the plant material must be mechanically broken down or cooked. Raw uncrushed plant material passes through the dog's simple digestive tract without being properly broken down, so these poorly digested, large carbohydrate molecules cannot be absorbed by the intestines. Even cooked plant material is relatively hard for a carnivore to digest. At the same time, cooking destroys many of the valuable plant nutrients.

The indigestible structural material found in plants, often referred to as fiber or roughage, is also a type of carbohydrate. Though fiber passes through the dog's digestive tract essentially unchanged, it nevertheless plays an essential role as it helps cleanse the intestines and promote proper elimination. Proper amounts of fiber also help regulate your dog's weight and nourish the beneficial bacteria and mucous membrane lining the digestive tract.

FATS

Providing fuel for metabolism, as well as a structural matrix for cells, fats are an essential part of your dog's diet. Fats provide your dog with energy, as well as certain vitamins and essential fatty acids, which are particularly important to the health of your dog's coat, skin, and inflammatory system. Fats also aid in the formation of prostaglandins, hormones, the functioning of the nervous system, and temperature regulation. Unfortunately, fat is also a storehouse for toxins.

Of the saturated fats, poultry fat seems to be the most digestible for dogs and also contains more essential fatty acids. Plant and fish fats, though not as concentrated a source of energy, are normally a better source of anti-inflammatory fatty acids than is animal fat. The amount of fat needed in a dog's diet depends on his age, lifestyle, and environment. Extremely active dogs and working dogs in cold climates need much more fat than do dogs in temperate areas. Older, less active dogs require less fat than their younger counterparts. Olive, canola, safflower, evening primrose, and flaxseed oils are all good sources of anti-inflammatory fatty acids for your dog, as are fish oils.

Although contributing to the palatability of your dog's food, fat is difficult to preserve in dog food. It often becomes rancid, which leads to the formation of toxins and free radicals that are responsible for tissue degeneration. Take care not to store large quantities of dog food for too long a time (no more than three or four weeks) without refrigerating or freezing it. Purchase your commercial, dry dog food from a store with a high turnover rate to ensure freshness. Foods using natural preservatives, such as vitamin E, should be purchased more frequently in smaller quantities. Freshness dates, telling the buyer just when the food was manufactured, are normally printed on the container and should be checked before the food is bought. Though canned food will keep for quite a long time, it's best to pay attention to expiration dates found on the can.

WATER

Your dog's body is composed of about 60 to 70 percent water. This essential nutrient must be consumed regularly by your dog in order to maintain proper cell metabolism, blood volume, and normal elimination functions. Insufficient amounts of water can result in dehydration and buildup of toxins, which unduly stress the liver and kidneys. A prolonged absence of water can lead to death. Tap water in many communities has been shown to be toxic, containing many harmful chemicals and heavy metals, such as lead, arsenic, or cadmium. Using a quality bottled water or filtration system is the only way to ensure a pure supply of water for yourself and your pets.

VITAMINS

Essential to maintaining proper cell metabolism, vitamins also ensure the healthy functioning of all systems in your dog's body. Aiding in the release of energy from digested food, vitamins play a role in blood production as well as the health of the skin and coat. Fat-soluble vitamins, such as A, D, E, and K, are stored in the dog's body for extended periods of time; oversupplementation with them can have toxic results. Water-soluble vitamins, such as B-complex and C, are not stored by the body (they are excreted through urine), and must be replaced on a regular basis.

Vitamins are found in both plant and animal foods. Some are even manufactured by bacteria found in your dog's intestinal tract (probiotics) or by his skin's reaction to sunlight (though this process is not nearly as pronounced as it is in humans). Because of the poor, depleted soil that most of our crops are grown in, many important vitamins and minerals are either missing from our crops or present in insufficient levels. Vitamin levels in lower quality commercial dog foods can also be depleted by overprocessing and lengthy storage times. To make up for this, manufacturers must fortify the food with added vitamins after processing has occurred. These added vitamins are rarely absorbed as well as those inherent to the original food source.

MINERALS

Necessary to the formation of bone and other tissues and the maintenance of proper cell metabolism, minerals are essential to your dog's diet. More than other essential nutrients, the level of mineral intake must be fairly precise; too little can result in the failure of metabolic functions, while too much can be toxic. Mineral deficiencies are commonplace among today's dogs, making proper supplementation a must.

Minerals important to your dog's health are divided into two categories, namely the *macrominerals* (which make up more than .01 percent of the total body weight) and the *microminerals* (which make up less than .01 percent of the total body weight). Any good-quality food should contain the following minerals to help meet the need as listed:

Macrominerals

- Carbon   Important for cell structure
- Calcium   Bone and teeth formation and nerve conduction

- Phosphorus   Cell metabolism
- Potassium   Cell metabolism
- Sulfur   Hair and skin health; formation of amino acids
- Sodium chloride   Maintenance of cellular pressure
- Magnesium   Cell metabolism
- Silicon   Formation and repair of connective tissues

Microminerals

- Iron   Oxygen transport and formation of hemoglobin
- Fluoride   Bone and teeth formation
- Zinc   Enzyme formation and skin health
- Strontium   Bone formation
- Copper   Enzyme regulation
- Cobalt   Metabolization of vitamin B_{12}
- Vanadium   Metabolization of fats
- Iodine   Thyroid regulation
- Tin   Unknown
- Selenium   Enzyme regulation; an antioxidant role
- Manganese   Enzyme regulation
- Molybdenum   Enzyme regulation
- Chromium   Glucose regulation

Though all minerals can be toxic in high doses, the following are particularly toxic and undesirable.

Minerals to Avoid

- Aluminum
- Arsenic
- Lead
- Mercury

- Beryllium
- Cadmium
- Antimony
- Barium
- Thallium
- Uranium

The National Academy of Science makes recommendations regarding the minimum daily requirements (MDR) for vitamins and minerals for humans and pets, obtained by determining amounts of nutrients needed to prevent a deficiency disease. Dog-food companies are required only to meet, but not exceed, these amounts. The MDR recommendations do not address the following concerns.

- The proper amounts of vitamins and minerals needed for "optimal health," not just the prevention of clinical disease or deficiency
- Ideal amounts of vitamins and minerals for treating existing diseases

In addition to receiving insufficient dosages of vitamins, a dog may suffer vitamin deficiencies brought on by undue stress or anxiety in his life.

Important Nonessential Supplements

Though not essential to maintaining your dog's life, the following substances (when used appropriately) may be beneficial to a dog suffering from various disorders, including infection, injuries, allergies, obesity, and advanced degenerative disease brought on by old age.

- Herbs/phytochemicals
- Probiotics (good bacteria)

- Digestive and antioxidant enzymes
- Nonessential amino acids, such as glycine, carnitine, and *N*-acetylcysteine
- Hydrochloric acid
- Glyconutrients, glucosamine and chondroitin sulfate

Malnutrition

Malnutrition is defined as any imbalance in an organism's diet that results in poor health. A dog may be malnourished if he has a deficiency or excess of calories or certain essential nutrients, is consuming toxins in his food, or has an imbalanced diet that results in poor digestion or absorption of his food. Again, the widespread use of herbicides, pesticides, hormones, and antibiotics, combined with severely depleted soil and overprocessing of foods, makes it increasingly difficult to obtain nutrient-rich, consistently healthy food. In addition, most dog-food packagers do not vacuum-seal their dog food bags, which allows oxidation to occur and results in a loss of fatty acids and vitamins and the formation of toxin-free radicals.

The poor formulation of a dog food also can cause malnutrition. Missing or deficient nutrients (or improper ratios of nutrients) can contribute to poor health. For example, copper added in overly high amounts can reduce the absorption of zinc, which further contributes to malnutrition. Foods containing too much refined sugar, flour, or poor-quality fats are relatively deficient in usable nutrients, which can also lead to malnutrition.

Toxic Dog Food

As stated in the preceding section, the food you feed your dog may have hidden toxins from many sources, all of which combine to create toxic conditions for your pet's liver, kidneys, and immune system. Improper storage of raw ingredients can contribute to putrefaction of meat, as well as mold buildup on grains that create poisonous substances called *mycotoxins*. Fats become rancid when stored too long without the addition of proper preservatives. Bacterial contamination of unfresh raw meat also occurs, creating potential health problems for a pet who eats it (though the canine digestive system is better designed to deal with this threat). During processing, the addition of chemical preservatives, coloring agents, and taste enhancers increase the likelihood of toxicity, and the use of high heat may actually convert some good substances into unhealthy ones.

Manufacturing processes like cooking the food or grain can result in nutrient loss. For instance, cooking ingredients at too high a temperature can create carcinogenic toxins in food and destroy or change fragile, heat-sensitive nutrients, such as fatty acids, vitamins, enzymes, and probiotics. Amino acids, the building blocks of protein, also may become less nutritional under the effects of high temperatures.

Toxic buildup in our pet food also is amplified by the position of an animal on the food chain. Contaminated plant materials are eaten by livestock in great quantities, which serves to concentrate and magnify the toxic chemicals in the feed. In addition, these livestock are treated with such chemicals as hormones, antibiotics, and parasiticides. When these animals are slaughtered and processed into dog food, all the toxins along the way are, in effect, focused in that one bag of food. Although malnutrition is the primary cause of disease and degeneration in your pet, the good news is that you can effectively prevent and reverse it by removing as many of the toxins as possible, while providing the optimal nutrition that will support the body's efforts at detoxification.

The Meat-Based Diet

First take a look at your dog's eating history. The domestic dog, *Canis familiaris,* evolved from wolf ancestors as a primarily carnivorous animal who consumed its prey. Both the wolf and domestic dog have relatively simple, short digestive tracts that are far better suited to digest meat than grains or plant material. Wolves and domestic dogs have identical dentition, with teeth shaped to tear and pull off flesh, and crack and pulverize bones, but poorly shaped to grind grain and plant material. Despite their domestication, dogs' organ systems are still designed to make meat the primary part of their diet. Meat provides your dog with a nearly complete amino-acid profile.

Nevertheless, the majority of animals killed by wolves and wild dogs are herbivores. Since canines eat the entire carcass (including the stomach, intestines, and everything within), they end up eating predigested plant material on a regular basis. Already broken down by the victim's digestive juices, the nutrients from this predigested plant material can be more readily utilized by the canine digestive tract. Though still largely a carnivore, your dog should be fed some plant material, provided it has been mechanically pulverized, grated, steamed, or sufficiently cooked to allow your dog's simple digestive tract to absorb its nutrients.

As more grain (even cooked) is fed to a dog, more undigested or partially digested grain protein collects in his upper small intestine. Within the dog's digestive tract, these large plant macromolecules are viewed as foreign substances that should not be there. The dog's intestinal immune system is alerted and tries to enzymatically destroy and remove these undigested molecules. Unfortunately, this enzyme also attacks the lining of the digestive tract, causing damage that results in a condition known as leaky gut syndrome, which I believe to be the origin of many disorders and diseases in humans and animals, including allergies, arthritis, and autoimmune diseases. (Note: See Step 6, pp. 127–151, for more on this.) As a supplementary source of nutrients, cooked grains are beneficial but should remain a minor part of the diet in relation to meat. Too high a percentage of grains in your dog's diet may cause nutritional deficiencies, and even create a host of immune-system related diseases.

The Superiority of a Natural Raw-Meat Diet

Over the past fifty years, veterinarians have seen a growing epidemic of chronic health problems. In my opinion, they coincide with the proliferation of improperly formulated commercial dog foods that may contain toxins. Typically filled with poor-quality ingredients that lack usable meat protein, enzymes, vitamins, minerals, and probiotics, most commercial foods are made predominantly of difficult-to-digest cereal grains and relatively small amounts of more easily digested meat. The meat is normally of inferior quality, and always cooked, making the food that much less usable for the dog. The canine body's intolerance of these ingredients is seen in an increasing variety of health problems, ranging from allergies and skin disorders to organ dysfunction.

As a result, many holistic veterinarians across the country are advocating dog owners change to a natural, raw-meat diet for their pets in place of commercial food. Far superior to commercial diets, the natural raw-meat diet uses fresh uncooked meat, healthy table scraps, lightly steamed or pulverized vegetables, cooked whole grains, and small amounts of fruit and dairy products. The use of raw ingredients (especially raw meat) provides the dog with amino acids in their uncooked, unaltered state, beneficial bacteria, active enzymes, essential fatty acids, natural vitamins, and easily absorbed (chelated) minerals—few of which are found in cooked foods. Feeding a natural raw-meat diet even once per week helps keep the dog healthier and revitalizes all of his organ systems, including the immune system, detoxification system, and antioxidant defense system.

Shopping for and preparing a natural raw-meat diet allows the owner to see, smell, and touch the raw ingredients going into the pet's meals. Home preparation of your dog's diet ensures that the food is fresh, free from rancid fats, moldy grains, animal excrement, by-products, preservatives, coloring agents, flavor enhancers, and fillers. This type of diet maximizes your dog's ability to fight disease and build his immune reserve, which often become severely depleted in dogs eating a cereal-based commercial food.

Preparing a natural, raw-meat diet requires more time and energy on the part of the owner. And the thought of feeding raw meat to a dog is a turnoff to many owners, who raise questions of bacterial contamination. Fortunately, the dog's relatively simple and powerful digestive tract can destroy most pathogenic bacteria. (The pH is much lower than it is in humans.) Consider again the wolf, whose diet consists of meat that is always raw. He never suffers from bacterial poisoning because his stomach acids, much more potent than human gastric juices, quickly render these microbes inactive. Because Salmonella is a public health hazard, I do not recommend feeding raw poultry. Care must always be taken to purchase quality meat from a responsible market. Also, immediately freeze any meat that is not to be used within an hour of purchasing. If you still have concerns about feeding raw meat to your dog, you can cook it lightly, leaving the inside rare. Or, you can soak the meat with diluted grapefruit-seed extract (available at health-food stores), which is recommended to reduce the likelihood of bacterial danger. It is possible that even rare-cooked meat may still harbor dangerous bacteria. However, it is my opinion that the health benefits of this type diet far outweigh the risks involved.

Some Basic Recipes for Homecooking

The following are guidelines and recipes formulated by Dr. Bill Pollak, a holistic veterinarian and friend whose clinic is in New York.

You can use these for feeding your dog a nutritious, natural, raw-meat diet. Feel free to experiment by adding or changing ingredients (for instance, cooked oats can be replaced by brown rice), but try to stay within the general framework with regard to ratios. The basic ingredients for creating a natural homecooked diet for your dog include:

MEAT

No less than 35 percent of the total daily diet should be raw meat. Beef, venison, lamb, or organ meats are all fine. Avoid raw pork, poultry, or rabbit, as these meats are more likely to contain Salmonella or parasites (worms) in the raw state. Cooked fish can also be used, though it tends to be expensive and can harbor many toxins. It should be used only on occasion and not every day, as it does not contain all the essential amino acids and fats that a dog needs.

VEGETABLES

Steamed carrots, broccoli, cabbage, brussels sprouts, leafy greens, zucchini, beets, potatoes, and most other vegetables are fine. Avoid peppers and tomatoes, as these can cause indigestion. Go easy on fruits. They are not readily digested, so try adding them a little at a time, in small pieces. Garlic is one of the best foods you can feed your dog; add it to every meal. Garlic intake should not exceed a quarter of a clove per 20-pound dog each day when fed on a routine basis. It has been shown that grating—and better yet, pulverizing—vegetables in a juicer is the best way to make plant nutrients available to carnivores.

GRAINS

Cooked brown rice, oats, wheat, buckwheat, barley, whole-grain bread, and whole-grain cereals are fine, but no more than 30 percent of the total diet should be grain (sprouted seeds are the most vital).

FATS

Olive, sesame, canola, safflower, and flaxseed are fine. These oils *must be refrigerated* and used up rapidly to avoid oxidation, which produces toxin free radicals.

DAIRY

Cheese, yogurt (with activated cultures), and cottage cheese are all fine. Egg yolks in their raw state also are a great source of nutrition; give your dog 1 or 2 eggs twice a week, depending on the size of your dog. Whole milk often causes diarrhea in dogs, so go easy on it.

BONEMEAL

To ensure that your dog gets adequate calcium, add 2–3 teaspoons of bonemeal to each serving of food (use human-consumption-quality).

Recipes

The following are balanced generic diets formulated for a midsized (40-pound), moderately active adult dog. Serve them once daily, substituting different types of raw meat, grains, and vegetables as described earlier.

Large batches can be made and frozen for several weeks if daily preparation is not feasible. Place mixtures in containers appropriate for daily ration size. Begin changeover from a commercial diet slowly, gradually reducing current diet while increasing the natural raw-meat diet over a 2-week period.

BASIC CANINE THREE-PART COMBO

¼ pound (½ cup) ground beef, lamb, or venson muscle meat— add liver not more than once weekly

4–6 slices whole, natural bread broken into small pieces, or pasta

1 cup whole milk

2 large eggs (shells crushed and baked at 350°F for 12 minutes)

¼ cup grated string beans or other vegetables

1 tablespoon multiple vitamin/mineral powder

1 tablespoon ghee, olive oil, or vegetable oil

1½ teaspoons bonemeal, calcium, or softened eggshells

200 IU vitamin E

Optional

¼ teaspoon tamari, Braggs liquid aminos, or a dash of iodized salt

½ clove garlic, crushed and minced

¼ teaspoon ginger, licorice, or cumin

Combine all ingredients. Water can be added. Serve raw or bake in a 325°F oven for about 20–30 minutes or until lightly browned.

CONTINENTAL CANINE

This recipe is quick, easy, and contains the 3 basic food groups of raw meat, grated vegetables, and cooked grain.

1 cup raw rolled oats

1½ tablespoons of kelp

3 eggs (shells crushed and baked at 350°F for 12 minutes)

1 teaspoon bonemeal or calcium/magnesium powder

½ cup cottage cheese

1 cup raw chopped meat (no rabbit or pork)

2 cups of water

Bring water to a boil. Add the raw oats, cover, cook two minutes, turn off the heat, let stand about 10 minutes. Stir in rest of ingredients. Mix in some brewer's or nutritional yeast, lecithin, or olive oil.

The diets described may be used for all stages of your dog's life. However, growing pups, dogs that are pregnant or nursing and highly active sporting and working dogs should receive approximately 50 percent more food than what is recommended for the average adult dog of the same weight. Less active or geriatric dogs may not require the full adult quantity. It is important that you weigh your dog weekly and regularly evaluate his overall condition so that you can adjust the amount of food fed daily to fit your dog's individual requirement. The total quantity of food fed to a pup should be divided into 3 equal feedings until the pup reaches 6 months of age, at which time you can reduce the number of daily feedings to 2. Continue feeding 2 meals a day until the pup is approximately 1 year old, at which time you will be able to cut down to a single meal each day.

Beneficial Supplements

In addition to feeding your dog these nutritious home-prepared meals, you may want to give him certain supplements each day to ensure optimal health and a long life. These supplements will bolster the immune and antioxidant defense systems, and are recommended whether you choose to feed an all-natural raw-meat diet or a commercial pet food. However, they are far more important when a commercial diet is the major source of nutrition. Below are listed what I believe to be a rough approximation of the daily supplemental dosages of the vitamins and minerals a 20-pound dog should receive in order to approach a state of optimal health. If your dog weighs 40 pounds, just double these recommendations. Use these figures as a rough goal. Do not worry about trying to match these exact numbers.

It will be impossible to find any one supplement that supplies all the following nutrients in the amounts recommended. Therefore my advice is that you begin by obtaining a high-quality, comprehensive vitamin/mineral supplement from your veterinarian. You can then add individual supplements or supplement combinations (available at the health-food store) in order to increase the quantity of each nutrient. These are recommended dosages necessary for optimal health and not the RDA (Recommended Daily Allowance), which is simply the amount necessary to prevent deficiency diseases. Make sure you check with your veterinarian before beginning this supplementation program.

VITAMINS

Fat-Soluble Vitamins

A 1500 IU (or the beta-carotene equivalent)
D 50 mg
E 100 IU
K 50 mcg

Water soluble Vitamins

B_1, thiamine	5 mg
B_2, riboflavin	5 mg
B_3, niacin	5 mg
B_5, pantothenic acid	5 mg
B_6, pyridoxine	5 mg
PABA	5 mg
Choline	100 mg
Inositol	50 mg
B_{12}, cobalamin	10 mcg
Biotin	60 mcg
Folic acid	80 mcg
B_{15}, pangamic acid	50 mg
Ascorbic acid (Vitamin C)	500 mg
Bioflavanoids	100 mg

MINERALS

Calcium	30 mg
Phosphorus	20 mg
Potassium	80 mg
Magnesium	30 mg
Molybdenum	30 mcg
Iron	15 mg
Zinc	5 mg
Copper	0.3 mg
Iodine	30 mcg
Selenium	30 mcg
Manganese	1.5 mg
Chromium	30 mcg
Sulfur	250 mg

HERBS AND PHYTOCHEMICALS

The following herbs are excellent sources of nutrients, antioxidants, and phytochemicals that can be used when needed to increase nutrition, aid in digestion, support the immune and detoxification systems, and encourage regeneration of tissues. They are not essential, but should be considered as possible additions to the diet in order to strengthen your pet's overall resistance to disease and to help her recover from a stressful situation or a disease process. What can't be found at a grocery store are available at health-food stores. A 20-pound dog should receive 1/5 the adult human dose recommended on the bottle.

Alfafa sprouts
Basil
Bee pollen
Brewer's yeast
Blue-green algae
Burdock root
Curcuma longa

Dandelion
Garlic
Gingko leaf
Ginseng
Horsetail
Kelp powder
Licorice root
Parsley
Spirulina
Thyme
Wheat grass

In addition to giving simply a vitamin/mineral supplement, consider giving one that includes fatty acids, amino acids, probiotics, and enzymes. Available at quality pet shops, veterinary clinics, and health-food stores, the addition of these supplements help ensure proper digestion and optimal metabolic function (especially helpful for the older dog, whose system may lack the digestive enzymes needed to properly extract these nutrients from food). Also, add a small amount (2 to 3 tablespoons) or probiotic nutrients each day, in the form of lactobacillus acidophilus yogurt or a lactobacillus capsule, to strengthen levels of beneficial bacteria in the dog's colon, as well as providing extra calcium and protein. And remember to include the aforementioned herbs and phytonutrients in your dog's diet.

A Feeding Alternative

If you feel that you don't have time to deal with the shopping and preparation that goes into a home-cooked diet, another viable option is to replace about 10 to 20 percent of your dog's commercial food with raw meat. Even this smaller portion of fresh, raw meat improves your dog's health tremendously. This feeding option can be used for puppies and adult dogs.

You can conveniently store each supplemental portion in a separate plastic bag, freeze, and thaw each when needed. Make enough for 7 to 10 feedings to keep daily preparation time to a minimum. When you mix raw meat into your dog's daily dry food, add some warm water and stir well. Also, add the same supplements that you would with the totally homemade diet. Vitamins, minerals, enzymes, amino and fatty acids, herbs, and phytonutrients, all available in easy-to-use powder form, are even more important to the dog eating a mostly commercial diet, as some key nutrients may be rendered useless or less effective due to processing procedures. Last, as with the home-cooked diet, once each day, give your dog 2 to 3 tablespoons of lactobacillus acidophilus yogurt or a lactobacillus capsule for essential probiotics, calcium, and protein, and 1 tablespoon of brewer's yeast for additional B-complex vitamins.

Choosing a Healthy Commercial Dog Food

A third option, for those who do not want to spend any time in the kitchen, is to choose a chemical-free, whole-grain commercial diet containing as much meat and as little grain as possible. For these owners, choosing a nutritious commercial food is an issue of great importance. The following section can help you decide what commercial food is best for your dog.

Above all, however, owners need to educate themselves in the area of canine nutrition by reading books and articles and talking with their veterinarians. Also essential is researching the dog-food companies that they are considering by evaluating all available company-provided pamphlets or by contacting the companies directly and asking to speak with their nutritionists. Several selection criteria apply when choosing a quality commercial dog food, including:

WHERE TO PURCHASE

Commercial outlets for dog food include supermarkets, pet stores, health-food stores, veterinary clinics, and mail order. Where you purchase the food has become less important of late, as some supermarkets now carry high-quality foods whereas many pet shops and other supposedly premium outlets also carry inexpensive, poor-quality products. Basically, you should choose a dog food according to its nutritional merits, and not according to where it's sold or its marketing slogan.

MEAT- OR GRAIN-BASED

Ingredients on dog-food packages are listed by order of weight, from highest to lowest. The first three ingredients on the list usually make up the bulk of the food. A meat-based diet (the most advantageous) is generally one that lists meat as the first two or three ingredients.

QUALITY OF MEAT USED

Always choose a food containing meat that has been inspected at a USDA slaughterhouse. Poor-quality dog foods often use meat from non-USDA rendering plants, where many of the animals used are either diseased, dead, or dying.

USE OF MEAT BY-PRODUCTS

Meat by-products may contain bones, feathers, fecal material, feet, beaks, heads, organs, and skin, and are therefore an unpredictable source of meat protein. Though some of these may be quite nutritious, others are not. Because no laws currently exist to force manufacturers to itemize exactly what meat by-products they use, staying away from these foods is a good idea.

The Cereal Portion

Often, the cereal portion of a dog food contains highly refined "fractions" of grain instead of cooked whole grains. Examples of grain products include peanut hulls, flour, gluten, and empty husks or "middlings." Whole grains are much more nutritious, so check for them on the label. Also, many dogs tend to be allergic to wheat and soy, so look for other grains such as rice and oats.

Chemical Preservatives, Coloring and Flavoring Agents, and Texturizers

Chemicals in dog food have been associated with both physical and behavioral problems. Cancer, reproductive problems, aggression, timidity, and obsessive-compulsive disorders are all problems that may be related to the presence of unwanted chemicals, including*:

- Fat preservatives such as ethoxyquin, BHT, BHA, and propyl gallate
- Moisturizers such as propylene glycol, calcium silicate, and sorbitol
- Stabilizers such as tartaric acid, citric acid, and salts of potassium
- Texturizers such as sodium nitrate and nitrite
- Mold retardants such as calcium and sodium propionatesorbic acid and sodium diacetate
- Coloring dyes that make the food more appealing to the pet owner

The most common natural fat preservatives are vitamins E and C. The drawback to using these, however, is that they do not preserve food for as long as the chemicals used in less-nutritional foods. For this reason, you should purchase dog food preserved with vitamins E and C more often, in lesser quantities.

*Although these substances are suspected of causing disease, conclusive evidence has not yet been established.

SOURCE OF FAT

Inferior fat, such as what comes from poor-quality animals, can lead to health problems. The best fat comes from animals who have been raised with little or no exposure to toxins, or from organically grown plant sources, which contribute essential omega-3 and omega-6 fatty acids. Old or improperly preserved fat can turn rancid, introducing toxins into the dog's body and degrading his health.

FRESHNESS

Every bag of dog food you purchase should have either the date of manufacture or an expiration date printed on it. If you cannot find this, do not buy the food. The date may be coded, so call the company if unsure. Buying from retailers who have a high turnover rate also ensures a fresher product. If the bag is stained, or if the food smells moldy or rancid, return it. Most manufacturers produce huge quantities of food all at once, and warehouse much of it for long periods. A few companies produce food in small quantities and much more frequently; therefore, food is much fresher, and rancidity is held to a minimum.

STATEMENT OF NUTRITIONAL COMPLETENESS

Look for a statement on the bag that says the food is "nutritionally complete." This guarantees that the food has been evaluated by feeding trials or lab testing and meets the minimum government requirements.

ADDED SUPPLEMENTS

The manufacturer's addition of chelated minerals, vitamin, fatty acids, enzymes, or probiotics to a food after the manufacturing process increases the food's nutritional value. Look for any statement to this effect on the bag or in the literature.

Dry, Canned, or Semimoist Meat?

Of the three types of dog food available, the dry versions can come close to providing your dog with the least toxic and most complete and balanced nutrition. They also are the least expensive. Semimoist, burger-type foods add moderate to high amounts of refined sugar, chemical preservatives, color enhancers, salt, and other chemical additives to aid in moisture retention and texture control. These ingredients have no beneficial health effects; to the contrary, they may be toxic, and may contribute to degenerative disease and aging.

Canned food comes in various qualities, from a primarily cereal-grain canned food to all-beef. It may be considered a complete and balanced food or just a food supplement, as with the all-beef variety. You should always look on the can for the AFFCO statement that the food is nutritionally complete, unless of course you are just looking for a food supplement, in which case such assurance is unnecessary. Canned food, though probably the most palatable, often falls short nutritionally. Most canned foods contain 60 to 75 percent water, making them much more expensive and less nutritious pound for pound. Additionally, canned food–only diets can contribute to faster tooth decay compared to dry food.

A viable alternative for owners with finicky eaters is to mix some high-quality canned food (available at pet shops) with a premium dry food. Though not as nutritious as adding fresh raw meat, the addition of the canned food makes the meal more palatable.

Misleading Packages

Unfortunately, much of the information we need for making an enlightened choice about which commercial dog food to buy is not printed on the bag or label. To make matters worse, much of what is on the label can be highly misleading.

The terms "premium" and "all natural" are often misleading. There are no laws determining their definitions; companies can therefore use them loosely to effectively market their product. Companies that buy ingredients, such as fat, that have already been preserved with a chemical like ethoxyquin do not by law have to list ethoxyquin as an ingredient of the food. This effectively hides the presence of this preservative from the consumer, allowing the company to claim that its food is "all natural."

The guaranteed analysis on the pet-food label provides useful yet minimal information, and can be ambiguous at best. The analysis percentages are based solely on the quantity of crude protein, fat, and carbohydrates, while offering no information on how much of these ingredients are actually usable and absorbable by the dog's system. Therefore, it is possible for a food with a high crude-protein amount, for example, to have less usable protein than a higher-quality food that lists a lower crude-protein percentage. In addition, the protein sources determine the types of amino acids present in the food: If the manufacturer uses protein sources providing an inferior or incomplete type of amino-acid profile, the dog suffers.

Dog-food manufacturers often manipulate the order of the ingredients listed in several ways. Grain ingredients are listed as separate fractions, rather than together as a single grain, in order to increase the likelihood that the meat ingredients are closer to the top of the list. In addition, nutritional analyses of food ingredients are done before processing and not after; this hides the fact that processing the ingredients always lowers nutritional values. And I have been told that in order to increase the apparent amounts of meat, for example, companies are allowed to weigh the meat used *before* the water is removed.

Finally, in order to truly compare and contrast nutrient percentages of canned food with dry or semimoist, you must first take into consideration only the *dry matter*. Canned food, for instance, is usually 75 percent water, which is equal to 25 percent dry matter. So, if the canned food label claims 8 percent protein, and the dry matter of the canned food is 25 percent, dividing 8 percent by 25 percent gives you the true percentage of protein available on a dry-matter basis, in this case 0.32, or 32 percent, a high percentage for a dog food. This can be done for all the other ingredients as well, including fat and carbohydrates. A dry dog food is almost all dry matter; therefore, the percentage of protein on the label is very close to its dry-matter percentage, so calculating the dry matter is unnecessary. Semimoist food is approximately 75 percent dry matter. You can use the same calculation methods for semimoist diets as you would with canned food.

The ideal food for your dog should prompt him to eliminate at least twice per day, with the stools being relatively firm, and not too odorous. If your healthy dog unexpectedly rejects a food that he has been eating regularly, perhaps the quality of the food has dropped. Perhaps the food is not fresh or has gone rancid. Also, you should suspect any food that your dog must eat in vast quantities just to maintain his body weight; it may have poor-quality (poorly digestible) ingredients. Finally, pay attention to how your dog's coat appears after he has eaten a food for a few weeks. It should appear lustrous and thick rather than dull and dry.

Step 6. Manage and Improve Your Dog's Internal Processes

What goes on inside your dog's body on a daily basis will largely determine not only how long he lives, but how well he lives. A dog who has improperly functioning digestive, detoxification, inflammatory, immune, or endocrine systems due to poor diet or lifestyle will suffer an abbreviated lifespan, and may contract many debilitating conditions that can make the quality of his life miserable. This step will explain how these important systems work and what can go wrong. In addition, the end of the section contains suggestions on how to get all your dog's systems to function better.

Digestion and Detoxification

Feeding your dog a proper, well-balanced diet means very little if its nutrients are not properly digested and absorbed into his system. Getting nutrients out of the food and into the cells of your dog's body should be one of your major goals, along with providing a high-quality diet and a safe, stress-free environment. Unfortunately, efficient digestion and absorption do not occur as easily as you might think, due to a number of factors:

- Genetic weakness
- Dietary deficiencies
- Disease and infection

- The effects of aging on the digestive system
- Environmental toxins that injure enzymatic actions in the dog's system
- Allergies and their effects on digestive, detoxification, and immune functions

You must bring your dog's digestive system to the healthiest, most nutrient-receptive state possible in order to guarantee proper metabolic function. Putting high-octane fuel into an old, beat-up jalopy won't make an old car last longer or run smoother; the vehicle must be in good running condition first.

DIGESTION

Your dog's digestive tract is designed to process and break down food into simple chemicals that can be absorbed into the bloodstream through the intestinal walls. When entering the mouth, food is mixed with saliva, making it easier to swallow. Saliva also begins the digestive process due to the actions of its digestive enzymes, which start to break down starches.

Once swallowed, food enters the stomach, where powerful gastric juices break it down. The dog's gastric juices (primarily hydrochloric acid) are normally quite efficient at this, provided that special cells in the stomach lining secrete them in sufficient quantities. Large protein, fat, and carbohydrate molecules are broken down, and vitamins and minerals are liberated, allowing everything nutritious to be utilized.

The broken-down food moves from the stomach to the small intestines, where enzymes from the pancreas, liver, and intestinal walls and bile from the gall bladder complete the digestive process and also neutralize potent stomach acids. Once the digestion process is complete, the usable nutrients are absorbed through the cell membranes of the mucosal lining of the intestines. When functioning properly, the mucosal lining easily discriminates between desirable and undesirable molecules. It prevents the absorption of potentially harmful compounds by binding various secreted anti-bodies to the unwanted substances, making them too large to diffuse through the intestinal cell membranes.

The large intestine functions to rid the dog's body of indigestible or undesirable substances and to absorb any available and needed water back into the system. Most of the probiotic material can be found here. Very important to the digestive process, these microbes help metabolize various nutrients, including fats, carbohydrates, and vitamins. These beneficial bacterial are of paramount importance in preventing the overgrowth of sinister forms of bacteria and yeast.

INADEQUATE DIGESTION AND MALABSORPTION

Numerous problems arising during the digestive process can ulti-mately lead to insufficient nutrient absorption or absorption of un-wanted toxic substances. When this occurs, your dog's overall health suffers, contributing to premature aging and a general de-generation of all body systems.

A dog with tooth or gum disease may have a sore mouth and may not want to eat, which results in malnourishment. The plaque that accumulates on her teeth and under her gums serves as a breeding ground for bacteria and their toxins, which are eventually absorbed into the general circulatory system and can move to the heart, kid-neys, liver, and lungs, where they can cause chronic organ diseases.

Insufficient amounts of stomach acid also can lead to significant health problems for your dog. Vital to the breakdown of food, a deficient amount of stomach acid can cause problems such as mal-nourishment, parasitic infections, malabsorption of vitamins and minerals, diarrhea, constipation, immune system overload, and al-lergies. The most common cause of a reduction in the volume of gas-tric secretions is advancing age; dogs over 8 to 10 years old, due to atrophy of the digestive tract, often suffer from this problem, which compounds the other health maladies that age can bring.

A growing number of holistic practitioners feel strongly that food allergies may be a leading cause of chronic disease and aging. Food allergies in your dog can be caused by improper digestion and malabsorption. As they age, dogs, like humans, can develop sensitivities to almost any type of food. Common allergens are grains, meats, or dairy products, but can be almost anything. Heredity, poor intestinal function, improper and excessive use of drugs, pollution, and limited exposure to different types of food may contribute to the appearance of a food allergy.

Once eaten, the food to which the dog is allergic is often not properly digested. This undigested material, upon coming into contact with the dog's intestinal lining, initiates an antibody reaction that causes inflammation and results in damage to the intestinal lining. Once the intestinal lining is damaged, the dog is less able to absorb essential nutrients. The damaged lining is also far more likely to allow the passage of large toxic molecules and bacteria directly into the bloodstream. Known as leaky gut syndrome, this disorder can cause severe autoimmune disease, more allergic reactions, arthritis, and a host of infectious illnesses.

Intestinal infections may occur when proper levels of any of the substances that normally prevent them, including stomach acids, intestinal enzymes, antibody secretions, and beneficial microbes, are reduced. Furthermore, yeasts, bacteria, or viruses may cause intestinal injury, resulting in inflammation, cell death, and malabsorption of nutrients. Parasitic infestations are a major cause of intestinal damage. Infection also can result from an allergic reaction, toxic substances, or autoimmune diseases, which can mistakenly cause the dog's immune system to attack its own digestive tract.

Dysfunction of the canine pancreas or liver can result in malabsorption of nutrients. Responsible for producing certain enzymes necessary for digestion, any reduction in pancreatic secretions due to disease or age can lead to inadequate digestion and absorption of nutrients, particularly fats, proteins, and fat-soluble vitamins. An aged or dysfunctional liver may be unable to produce sufficient quantities of bile, which, along with dietary fiber, is responsible for transporting toxins out of the digestive tract.

Herbicides, pesticides, growth hormones, antibiotic and chemical preservatives, and food additives (all present in our food supply) can damage the canine intestines, poison the body, cause poor health, and lead to a shortened life span. They must be eliminated from your dog's environment when possible.

The increase in the production of free radicals in your dog's system, caused either by external pollutants or internal metabolic waste products, causes an oxidative overload that damages the digestive tract and all other organs. This process occurs most frequently as the dog ages; without a proper increase in dietary antioxidant supplementation, the dog's overall health declines.

YOUR DOG'S DETOXIFICATION SYSTEM

Besides making sure your dog is fed a superior diet that provides all the nutrients her body needs to function optimally, you must minimize and reduce toxins, one of the major causes of degenerative diseases. Nearly identical in form and function to your own system, your dog's detoxification system is designed to deactivate and excrete toxins from the body. Consisting primarily of the liver, gall bladder, intestines, and kidneys, a healthy detoxification system is vital to a long, healthy life.

The liver, an organ second in importance only to the brain and the heart, is the crucial player in the detoxification game. Tremendously versatile, its functions are numerous. The liver filters all the blood that leaves the gastrointestinal tract, removing harmful toxins that originate from environment and diet, normal metabolic processes, or intestinal bacteria. A complex series of enzymatic actions occurs to neutralize harmful toxic compounds such as environmental pollutants, histamines, unneeded hormones, bowel toxins, food additives, and many drugs, including aspirin and antibiotics. The liver also removes unwanted substances by producing bile, a substance that acts as a transport medium for moving toxins from the liver into the intestines and finally out of the body in the stool.

It is important to understand that all blood that goes through the intestinal tract picking up nutrients and toxins passes first through the liver before going back into the general circulatory system. If this blood, potentially loaded with all manner of toxins, went into the general circulation before the liver had a chance to filter and cleanse it, tissues and organs would undergo rapid damage, causing degenerative disease at a relatively young age. When significant liver damage occurs, allergies, arthritis, kidney disease, and auto-immune diseases are more likely to develop.

The kidneys also play a major role in detoxification. Responsible for blood filtration and the excretion of waste and excess water in the form of urine, the kidneys purge all toxins sent to them by the liver, which has made them water soluble.

DISORDERS OF THE DETOXIFICATION SYSTEM

Numerous internal and external forces can reduce the efficiency of your dog's detoxification system, creating a toxic internal environment that can damage your dog's health and shorten her life span. Nutritional deficits, genetic disease, excessive toxin exposure, and bile deficiencies or obstructions can all result in decreasing the liver's ability to detoxify the blood, resulting in degeneration in other organs.

Even when the liver is working normally and its detoxification mechanisms are healthy, avoidance of toxins is probably the most efficient and intelligent way to enhance your dog's overall health and help her reach a ripe old age. As long as a healthy liver can handle the toxins introduced to your dog's body, health continues. As soon as the toxin load exceeds the liver's abilities, degenerative disease begins. Consequently, avoiding toxins and conserving your dog's liver reserves makes great sense.

Although your dog constantly encounters toxins from the air, water, and food she takes in and from the metabolic waste products they produce, an unhealthy digestive system is probably the most damaging source of toxins. Toxins that injure the intestine and produce leaky gut syndrome (including allergens, bacterial infections, and nonsteroid anti-inflammatory drugs) are capable of exhausting your dog's liver. *Intestinal dysbiosis,* an overgrowth of certain yeast and bacteria that normally inhabit the intestinal tract in smaller numbers, can also generate toxins and allergens, altering the dog's ability to absorb nutrients. The overuse of antibiotics and the development of antibiotic-resistant yeast and bacteria are the primary causes of intestinal dysbiosis.

Poisonous chemicals, unnecessary chemical food additives, contact with herbicides, pesticides, and toxic plant materials from your pet's environment are major causes of an overload of your pet's detoxification system. A result of the industrial world we live in, these substances have become increasingly hard to avoid.

GIVING THE LIVER A HELPING HAND

As your pet's primary detoxifier, her liver must be in top working order at all times. You can help maintain its effectiveness (and even increase its capabilities somewhat) by reducing the liver's exposure to toxins, stimulating excretion of toxins from the liver, supporting the liver's detoxification enzyme system, and reducing fat build-up in the liver.

Reduce free-radical damage to the liver by ensuring proper antioxidant intake. Vitamins C and E, bioflavonoids, carotenoids, glutathione, and selenium are very important as free-radical scavengers.

Provide your dog with sufficient amounts of lecithin (available at health-food stores) and feed her at least 1 or 2 raw eggs each week. Both of these substances contain *phospholipids,* a type of fat that helps protect the liver from organic solvents.

Supplement your dog's diet with milk thistle seed, which fights free-radical buildup and helps protect the liver from toxins (available in health-food stores). Adjust dosages according to weight; for a dog of forty or more pounds, 50 mg is a good starting point. (Note: consult your vet before administering any supplements to your dog. See also the section entitled *The Plan: A Year in the Life of Your Dog* for more information on dosages.)

Promote adequate bile production by sprinkling the spice turmeric on your dog's food at least once each week. Also occasionally feed her cooked dandelions (including the roots) or artichoke leaves.

Protect the liver from fat buildup by decreasing the amount of saturated fats, increasing water-soluble fiber, and providing lipotropics, such as choline, methionine, carnitine, and vitamin B_{12}.

Stimulate the liver's detoxification mechanism by supplying glycine and sulfur-brassica foods (such as cabbage, cauliflower, brussels sprouts, and broccoli), supplemented with the antioxidant enzyme glutathione. Provide a multivitamin supplement, especially when disease is present.

The Inflammatory and Immune Systems

Your dog's body constantly repairs and discards damaged tissues while fighting off uncountable toxins and invaders attempting to use and abuse all of its systems. The dog's body has the natural capacity to protect and maintain itself, as long as circumstances are optimal. The *inflammatory* and *immune systems,* remarkable in design and function, serve to repair, maintain, and protect your dog's body from unseen harm, provided they are maintained through both nutrition and proper lifestyle habits.

Unfortunately, we live in an increasingly toxic world that places an inordinate strain on these miraculous systems, and in the process inhibits their effectiveness. The nutrient-poor, toxin-containing commercial diets that we have been feeding our dogs for the last forty to fifty years, combined with a rise in infectious agents, magnify the strain on both of these watchdog systems. Many dogs begin to suffer serious health problems, resulting in shortened life spans.

This section explains how the inflammatory and immune systems work, and how they can be compromised and damaged.

THE INFLAMMATORY SYSTEM

Important as a housecleaning and repair system, your dog's inflammatory system is a self-regulating "maintenance crew" that makes healing possible. Your dog's body regularly suffers tissue damage due to injury, infections, toxins, malnutrition, and cellular aging. This damage occurs in the cells, which then need to be removed and replaced. Any type of cell damage elicits a response through the release of chemicals such as *histamines* and *prostaglandins.* The release of histamines, prostaglandins, and other chemicals that occurs during more substantial incidences of cellular damage serves to increase blood flow to the damaged tissues through the dilation of blood vessels. This dilation causes an increased localized rise in temperature and a reddening of the skin, which is why the injured area actually feels warm to the touch. The affected area also becomes swollen due to an increased permeability of the capillaries that allows fluid to seep out of the vessel and into the surrounding tissue. The swelling immobilizes the damaged area while allowing for the rapid passage of nutrients and white blood cells to the site of tissue injury.

The chemicals released during this process lure in the white blood cells, which then go about the job of engulfing and destroying unwanted microorganisms and removing toxins and damaged tissues. When the damage or infection is serious, the affected area becomes a virtual battlefield, replete with chemical warfare agents, soldiers, invaders, and tensely fought battles. When all works properly, the "good guys," namely your dog's inflammatory and immune systems, wins.

Once this inflammatory fracas has run its course and the bad guys have been eliminated, cellular repair and tissue regeneration begins. A constantly occurring process, the body quickly breaks down into a state of total disrepair without it. Unfortunately, things do not always work according to plan.

WHAT CAN GO WRONG

Balancing the degree and location of the inflammatory response is a complex and tricky procedure that may sometimes go haywire, resulting in damage to healthy tissues or an unregulated, unchecked inflammatory response that leads to chronic inflammatory conditions and overall failing health. Conditions such as arthritis, allergies, inflammatory bowel disease, leaky gut syndrome, cancer, and serious autoimmune diseases appear in dogs as a result of a malfunctioning, overstimulated, exhausted inflammatory system. A number of factors can cause your dog's inflammatory process to either overreact or become depressed, causing damage and degeneration in healthy tissues, including:

Improper Diet

A number of poor dietary formulations can initiate an undesirable inflammatory response in your dog. Special regulatory molecules called *prostaglandins* are made from essential fatty acids deprived primarily from diet. They are responsible for initiating, supporting, and mediating the inflammatory response. An imbalance in these fatty acids can lead to improper inflammatory response.

A diet deficient in *essential omega-3 fatty acids* (derived from fish, flaxseed, evening primrose, or linseed oils) will not promote the formation of the *anti-inflammatory prostaglandins*, essential in limiting the inflammatory response. Many commercial dog foods contain little or no omega-3 oils and instead use saturated, hydrogenated, or cooked oils, which allow unchecked inflammation to occur.

Deficiencies in other nutrients can promote hyperactive inflammation in several ways. A deficiency of vitamins C and E, zinc, magnesium, and beta-carotene may results in a shortage if several enzymes needed to convert fatty acids into anti-inflammatory prostaglandins.

Dog foods containing high levels of chemical additives, herbicides, hormones, or antibiotics also may cause the inflammatory system to become hyperactive. Perhaps most importantly a lack of antioxidants in your dog's diet may cause healthy cells to become more vulnerable to harsh oxidizing chemicals released during the inflammatory process. A dietary deficiency of carotenoids from vegetables and flavonoids from fruit (both important in mediating and stabilizing the inflammatory response) promotes unchecked, destructive inflammation.

A diet that contains foods to which your dog is allergic triggers the inflammatory process, causing eventual damage to healthy cells lining your dog's intestine. A poor overall diet weakens your dog, lowering his ability to fight off infection and illness. Once ill, a dog's inflammatory system becomes activated; if the dog is constantly sick, the inflammatory response never stops and becomes overstimulated, causing widespread damage, rather than repair, in many areas of the dog.

Environmental Toxins and Pollutants

Contaminated food, water, soil, and air in your dog's environment can hyperactivate his inflammatory system. These foreign substances are treated like invading bodies, triggering the inflammatory (and immune) response. When these toxins are encountered, your dog's inflammatory process is activated and often overworked. One example of this is intestinal dysbiosis, which acts as an internal source of toxicity.

Advancing Age

The aging dog, having encountered a toxic burden over a long time period, tends to suffer more from inflammation (and the resulting pain) than a younger, healthier dog. The older dog's systems, more vulnerable to infection, disease, and leaky gut syndrome, typically experience more inflammatory responses than do a younger animal's. In addition, degeneration of the intestinal lining and a decrease in stomach acid and pancreatic enzyme production all contribute to maldigestion and malabsorption.

Stress

Any dog undergoing high levels of emotional and psychological stress is more susceptible to illness. Once ill, the inflammatory process begins; if stress is constant, the dog's body is constantly subjected to disease and a hyperactive inflammatory process, which contributes to widespread cellular damage and further loss of health.

Illness or Injury

An otherwise healthy dog who suffers some type of chronic illness or injury experiences a prolonged, hyperactive inflammatory response. A serious viral infection or injuries sustained from being hit by a car, for instance, can provoke the inflammatory system into overreacting, eventually causing system-wide damage to otherwise healthy cells. Prolonged illness further stimulates the inflammatory response due to the high degree of oxidative cellular damage resulting from free-radical buildup.

Improper Drug Use

Overuse of certain drugs can cause the inflammatory process in your dog to underreact or overreact. Cortisone, for example, used as an anti-inflammatory, can result in a system-wide increase in pathogens that actually stimulate the inflammatory process, especially when cortisone treatment stops. Aspirin, acetaminophen, and ibuprofen may create similar consequences if misused. Excessive use of antibiotics can cause internal dysbiosis, which overstimulates the inflammatory process and also creates a mechanism for harmful microbes to become resistant to the same antibiotics that were designed to kill them. This mechanism allows the new, resistant microbes to proliferate, further taxing all of the dog's defense systems.

The Immune System

Responsible for locating, destroying, and removing potentially harmful invaders from your dog's body, the immune system is complex, well orchestrated, and extremely responsive to any substance that does not belong. It is truly one of the vital keys to good health and long life.

When an invading pathogen, toxin, or allergen manages to get past your dog's skin or mucosal membranes, the immune system goes into action. Different types of protective white blood cells travel to the point of invasion and attack. The invaders, called *pathogens* or *allergens*, provoke a three-part immune response. In response to a pathogen, the body first increases production of mucus by the mucus membranes, which entraps the invading substance and keeps it from getting through the membranes of the respiratory and digestive tracts. In the mucus are antibodies that bind with the pathogens and prevent them from penetrating through the mucus membrane and into the bloodstream. The cells of the mucus membrane further defend against invasion by acting as a mechanical barrier to invasion.

If the invading pathogen manages to get through this first line of defense, an inflammatory response, also known as the cell mediated defense, goes into action. This inflammatory response brings in specific defense cells known as *neutrophils* to attack the foreign substance and destroy it.

During the battle of the neutrophils, many pathogens are injured or killed and parts of their internal structure seep out and act as *antigens,* which stimulate the third line of defense known as the *humoval defense.* This defense system consists of two types of white blood cells. The *B lymphocytes* secrete *antibodies,* which attach onto the antigens and make it easy for the second type of white cell, the *macrophage,* to identify the foreign invader. The macrophage then engulfs the invader and enzymatically devours it. When working properly, the various types of specialized immune cells maintain a careful balance in your dog's system, attacking only harmful substances and avoiding beneficial "visitors" such as well-digested nutrients or beneficial, health-producing bacteria.

What Can Go Wrong

To keep his immune system in good working order, your dog must be in good health, take in proper nutrients, and avoid immune-suppressing toxins and mental stressors. Many factors come into play, however, that may damage or suppress your dog's immune system and lead to prolonged illness, poor health, and a shortened life span. Other factors cause an overstimulation of the immune and inflammatory systems, which results in allergies, arthritis, and auto-immune diseases.

Nutrient Deficiencies

The food your dog receives each day helps fuel the many complex workings of its immune system. A deficiency in one or more essential nutrients can lead to immune dysfunction, and open the dog up to infection and illness, leading to a shortened life span. Deficiencies in any or all of the following nutrients will undermine the function of your dog's immune system and open the way for illness:

- Vitamin A
- B-complex
- Vitamin C
- Vitamin E
- Selenium
- Zinc
- Fatty acids

In addition to specific deficiencies, dogs who are simply malnourished or obese also may suffer decreased immune-system function through either deficiencies in essential nutrients, or in the case of the obese dog, the excess presence of certain types of lipids, which can inhibit or overstimulate immune response. Also, high quantities of refined sugar in your dog's diet may reduce the efficiency of both neutrophil and lymphocytic white cells. (Sugar decreases the ability of neutrophils to destroy bacteria, whereas starch, a more complex carbohydrate, has no such immune-suppressing characteristics.)

Toxins and Allergens

The many toxins your dog's system must deal with, both internally and externally, can either overstimulate or suppress the immune system, resulting in symptoms ranging from autoimmune disease to chronic infection. Food allergens can and do cause overstimulation of the immune system when it views overly large protein molecules as harmful invaders.

Pesticides, herbicides, preservatives, and other food additives, as well as numerous drugs (particularly cortisone, aspirin, and other anti-inflammatory medications, certain antibiotics, and cancer treatment drugs), may act as powerful immune system suppressants, inhibiting the actions of the white blood cells and causing dysfunction of the lymphatic system. Heavy metal contamination from substances such as lead, cadmium, mercury, arsenic, nickel, and aluminum causes severe and permanent damage by retarding antibody formation and white-blood-cell function. Also damaging to your dog's immune system are common household chemicals such as cleaners, solvents, paint thinner, gasoline, antifreeze, and motor oil.

Infection and Injury

Trauma and illness severely tax your dog's immune system, as well as the inflammatory and antioxidant defense systems. A long-standing infection activates the immune system nonstop, causing an eventual exhaustion or "burnout." Serious injuries or surgery also may have this effect.

Stress

Illness resulting from chronic stress and anxiety is a very real phenomenon. Anything that causes your dog to feel anxious, insecure, or frightened (which depends largely on your dog's personality and temperament) may cause damage to his immune system. When a dog becomes uneasy or frightened, his body's biochemistry prepares for some sort of looming trauma. This fight-or-flight response diverts the dog's metabolic energies to his muscles. Hormones decrease white-blood-cell function and shrink the thymus, perhaps the most important immune system gland of the body. Lymphocytes, the body's natural killer cells, are reduced in number, decreasing the immune response.

Yeast and Bacterial Imbalances

The yeast *Candida* is a normal inhabitant of the digestive tract. However, prolonged antibiotic therapy, cortisone therapy, or excessive amounts of simple carbohydrates may stimulate an overgrowth of Candida that causes damage to the intestinal mucosal lining. Such a yeast overgrowth, with its accompanying intestinal damage, causes an immune-system suppression.

Signs that your dog's immune system is malfunctioning or overworked include:

- Recurring, chronic, or frequent infections or disorders
- Slow-healing wounds
- Cancer
- Fatigue
- Elevated or suppressed white-blood-cell count
- Underactive thyroid gland (indicated by a blood test)

Hormonal Output and Cellular Regeneration

Any book about life extension for dogs would not be complete without touching on the importance of the endocrine system, as well as the process of cellular regeneration, both vital to ensuring optimal bodily functions. The endocrine system, responsible for producing metabolism-controlling hormones, profoundly influences all of the processes in your dog's body. Likewise, the ability of canine cells to regenerate for as long as possible is vital to all metabolic functions.

Hormones, like the software used in a computer, tell the dog's body what to do and how to react. In comparison, the cellular regenerative process maintains the "hardware," or the body itself. This section focuses on these two processes, what can go wrong with them, and how you can optimize each to improve your dog's health and extend her life span.

THE CANINE ENDOCRINE SYSTEM

Your dog's endocrine system is a collection of glands that manufacture and release hormones, the chemicals responsible for regulating metabolism, sexual development and function, stress response, temperature, growth, and a host of other functions. Basically a chemical messenger service, your dog's endocrine system serves to translate messages from the brain into actual metabolic functions. The glands of the endocrine system release their hormones directly into the bloodstream, which transports them to various locations throughout the body. For example, if your dog's sensory organs detect that some type of danger is approaching, they supply this information to the brain, which signals the adrenal glands, which then begin to produce and release *epinephrine* (also called *adrenaline*) into the dog's bloodstream, allowing the animal's musculoskeletal, cardiovascular, and respiratory systems to gear up and respond appropriately in either a fight-or-flight manner. The hormonal output of the adrenal glands, in other words, prompts the dog into defensive action.

The hormones produced by your dog's glands control every aspect of healthy functioning, from respiration and heartbeat to bone density and reproduction, and even appetite and temperament changes. The glands making up your dog's endocrine system include:

- Adrenal glands
- Hypothalamus
- Pancreas
- Parathyroid glands
- Pituitary gland
- Thyroid gland
- Ovaries (in females)
- Testes (in males)
- Pineal gland

WHAT CAN GO WRONG

Some hormones affect specific areas of your dog's body, whereas others affect many systems simultaneously. If the output of hormones becomes unbalanced, the health consequences can be dire. Some disorders that arise from a malfunctioning endocrine system include fatigue, hair loss, aggression, obesity, anorexia (which is different from the human, psychologically based disease), arthritis, blood disorders, cancer, diabetes, and maldigestion or malabsorption. If one or more glands malfunction, your dog's metabolism and health can suffer enormously, resulting in a shortened life span.

Many conditions arise that may inhibit proper functioning of the endocrine system. Toxins and pollution in the environment, poor diet, stress, infection and other diseases, or injuries can all be significant causes of glandular dysfunction, as can hereditary or congenital factors. An autoimmune disease or a tumorous growth on or near any of the glands may have particularly harmful effects on glandular output. Unchecked free-radical buildup and its degenerative effects also play a major role in damaging the endocrine system. Aging itself plays a major role in the slow, inexorable atrophy of all the glands and their functions.

Cellular Regeneration

Your dog's body is constantly generating new cells to replace the ones that die. A natural process, this repair-and-replace function remains fairly constant throughout your dog's life. When the number of damaged or dying cells begin to outnumber the quantity of replacement cells and the efficacy of repair, the dog begins to slow down and, in our eyes, age. Dogs suffering from excessive tissue damage combined with inadequate repair-and-replace function age faster than those who are able to repair and replace cells at the preferred rate.

CAUSES OF CELL DEGENERATION

Your dog may suffer degenerative damage to his various tissues in many ways, some more obvious than others. These can include:

- Injury
- Illness and infection
- Improper diet
- Toxins
- Allergies
- Stress
- Free-radical buildup
- Malfunctioning immune and inflammatory systems
- Inadequate rest
- Overactivity

How to Improve All of Your Dog's Internal Processes

Preventing poor digestion and absorption, impaired detoxification, excess inflammation, poor or excessive immune response, improper hormonal output, and sluggish cellular regeneration involves minimizing damaging conditions, avoiding harmful substances, and supporting any and all conditions that might help promote optimal metabolic response. All of these undesirable conditions can be minimized by following these guidelines:

- Make your dog's environment as safe as possible by avoiding potentially harmful situations. Avoiding contact with aggressive or sick animals and safeguarding the home are essential steps toward creating a safe environment. Realizing that an older dog is less athletically capable helps prevent injuries that tax the aging animal's regenerative processes. The fewer injuries, the less need for major cellular repair and replacement. Eliminate all toxins or dangerous conditions present (see Step Four). Keep your dog away from the road when off-leash, and get him trained!

- See the vet at least once a year to ward off or treat illnesses that could interfere with proper internal processes. Judicious use of vaccines also help prevent life-threatening illnesses from damaging your dog's regenerative powers. When your dog reaches eight years of age, consider seeing the vet at least twice a year for immune evaluation, nutritional consultation, and a physical exam. Also, ensure that your dog's teeth and gums are kept in the best condition possible by having your vet examine and clean them at least once a year. This simple precautionary step helps prevent harmful oral bacteria buildup, which can damage the gums, liver, heart, and kidney.

- Make sure that the food you feed your dog is nutritious and easily digestible. Meat is much easier for dogs to completely digest than are grains and vegetables, and should be the major component of the diet. Difficult-to-digest food serves as a poor source of nutrients and an irritant to the digestive tract. Providing a highly digestible meat-based diet (preferably raw) eliminates the burden placed on the dog's immune system by a diet consisting mostly of grain and other hard-to-digest food.

- Ensure that your dog receives all essential vitamins and minerals, key ingredients in supporting her ability to repair and replace damaged and dying cells. This becomes even more important in the older dog, who needs all the help she can get to keep up with the rigors of cell repair and replacement. Your pet must receive the nutrients she needs as they are most vital for keeping all systems functioning properly. Vital nutrients for a responsive metabolism include:
  - Vitamins A, B-complex, C, D, E, and K
  - The minerals copper, iron, manganese, magnesium, selenium, and sulfur
  - Beta-carotene and flavonoids (found in orange and yellow fruits and vegetables)
  - Foods rich in omega-3 fatty acids (including fish, linseed, flaxseed, and evening primrose oils)
  - Essential amino acids
  - Fiber and complex carbohydrates
- Normalize function by maintaining the proper balance of fatty acids in your dog's diet to support the formation of necessary regulating hormones. Adding omega-3 and omega-6 fatty acids in the form of fish oil or flaxseed helps accomplish this. In addition, supplement your dog's food with vegetables that are rich in beta-carotene as well as flavonoids. Fresh fruits, cooked carrots, broccoli, brussels sprouts, artichokes, and squash should therefore be included in your dog's daily diet.
- Avoid overfeeding your dog, which leads to obesity, one cause of immune system dysfunction.
- The older dog should receive more fiber in his diet to help remove toxins from his increasingly permeable intestinal lining. Daily

supplementation with *lactobacillus acidophilis* (two or three ta-blespoons) aids in keeping the bowel action normalized and helps reduce harmful microbes in that area. Make sure you take the older dog to the vet at least twice a year. Older dogs or those suffering from disease or nutritional deficiency may experience a drop-off in the amount of hydrochloric acid their stomachs pro-duce, which can lead to incomplete digestion of food and its as-sociated problems. First, identify whether the problem exists by carefully observing your dog's habits. If you notice changes in ap-petite, elimination habits, or general behavior, see your vet. Tests can determine if HC1 production in the dog's stomach is down. Often the first step in treatment is supplementation with the mineral zinc. A deficiency in this key mineral can result in a decrease in HC1 output as well as a loss of appetite. Zinc sup-plementation quickly and effectively cures the problem. In addi-tion to zinc, herbal bitters (available at health-food stores) can help stimulate and improve production of HC1. Available in liquid form, a few drops (masked in a treat) given a few minutes before the dog's bowl is placed on the floor can go a long way to improve digestion. If these supplements do not effectively restore your dog's decreased HC1 levels, your vet may prescribe HC1 supplementation as a means of restoring proper acidity and di-gestive capacity. Easy-to-use tablets or capsules are adminis-tered with each meal. (Note: HC1 supplementation must be discussed with your vet before implemented, as should dosages.)

• Along with a decrease in the production of HC1 in the stomach, the older dog may also begin to suffer from a decreased output of pancreatic enzymes, contributing to incomplete digestion and poor absorption of nutrients in the intestines. Symptoms of pan-creatic insufficiency include undigested fat in the stool, increased stool volume, and loose stool. Fortunately, once pancreatic insuf-ficiency is diagnosed, your vet can prescribe enzyme supplements derived from plant sources, particularly the fungus *Aspergillus oryzae.* Supplements that contain the enzymes lipase, protease, and amylase can restore proper digestive enzyme function.

- Supplement your dog's diet at least once a week with herbs and other supplements (available at health-food stores) that help support a healthy immune system, such as aloe vera, kelp powder, garlic, ginseng, goldenseal, echinacea, milk thistle, shiitake mushroom, astralagus, plant-derived proteolytic enzymes, and thymus extract.

- Ensure that the formation and accumulation of damaging free radicals are kept to a bare minimum by providing your dog with the proper antioxidant supplementation, particularly vitamins C and E, the minerals copper, iron, manganese, magnesium, selenium, and zinc, and beta-carotene, flavonoids, and garlic. Feeding the best and freshest diet possible to your dog also helps her body produce the powerful antioxidant enzymes superoxide dismutase (SOD), catalase, and glutathione peroxidase.

- Remove as many allergens as possible from your dog's environment and food to prevent excess cell degeneration and to allow regeneration to occur more effectively. Determining if your dog is allergic to any types of food also helps prevent any damage to the intestines. By paying careful attention to your dog's short-term and long-term reactions to the consumption of different foods and by working closely with your vet, you can learn if your dog is sensitive to certain foods. Then, simply avoid these troublesome ingredients to help your dog's digestive tract and immune system stay healthy. A pet who shows physiological or behavioral changes after eating beef or wheat, for instance, might remain symptom-free if you simply change over to chicken and oats or lamb and rice.

- Design your dog's life to be as stress-free as possible to free up energy that can be directed toward cell regeneration. Do not hit or yell at him, and avoid any potential for conflict, especially with aggressive animals. Do not put your dog into chaotic situations, especially if he is shy and timid by nature. Avoid leaving your dog alone for long periods of time, an unnatural condition for a pack animal. Give your dog a five minute daily massage to help reduce stress and make him content.

- Ensure that your dog gets enough sleep and rest, which provides the time for regeneration to occur. As your pet ages, this becomes more crucial. If your older dog wants to sleep more, let her. Puppies also need to sleep more than adults, as they constantly undergo profound cellular growth.

- Exercise your dog to promote and enhance metabolism, which will contribute to a more efficient repair and replacement process. The older dog can particularly benefit from exercise, due to the stimulating effects it has on the metabolism. Make sure not to overdo exercise, however, as this can injure the dog's body and tax its ability to repair and replace cells.

- Try to avoid the use of drugs as much as possible, as they may unnecessarily stimulate or depress the inflammatory and immune systems. Rely on the advice of your vet for giving medications when no other options are available.

- Prevent viral and bacterial infections and parasitic infestations (i.e., worms) in your dog's digestive tract to maintain vigorous digestion and absorption process. To prevent parasitic infestations, try to:
  - avoid feeding of raw pork or rabbit, as they may contain worms and other damaging parasites
  - keep your dog free of fleas, as they can carry tapeworms
  - avoid allowing your dog to drink directly from ponds or stagnant water
  - keep your dog away from the stools of other dogs
  - keep your dog's environment clean and parasite-free by regularly washing its blankets and doghouse, treating for fleas, and vacuuming daily
  - have your dog's stool checked every 4 months
  - keep sick or parasitized animals away from your dog

If you suspect any type of viral or bacterial infection in your dog, see your vet as soon as possible. Goldenseal can be used to treat bacterial infections, licorice root can be used for viral infections, and tea tree oil is good for fungal infections.

- Help eliminate bad bacteria from the digestive tract by supplementing the diet with garlic, a nutritious herb that helps eliminate bad bacteria (without harming the good types) and also acts as an efficient antioxidant. Additional supplementation with goldenseal, an herb available at health-food stores, will help kill bacteria and can sometimes be used along with echinacea as a replacement for antibiotics.

- Supplement your dog's diet with foods that help promote the growth of good bacteria. Small amounts of active-culture yogurt, banana, cooked asparagus, or cooked artichokes each week can accomplish this, as can adequate amounts of fiber, which serves as food for these beneficial bacteria.

- Periodic fasting appears to help in the regeneration of intestinal tissues and the intestinal mucosal lining and also seems to help evacuate intestinal toxins and allergens. To that end, perhaps once or twice per month consider putting your dog on a diet limited to one cup of brown rice, water, and vitamin/mineral supplements for a maximum of two to three days. If you so choose, you can even limit her diet to water or fruit juice and a vitamin/mineral supplement only, for no longer than two days. Never put your dog on a prolonged fast, especially if she is a very small dog, as her reserves are far less than yours or those of a large dog. Extended fasts can damage the intestinal lining, create leaky gut syndrome, and cause severe depletion of the body's nutrients.

PART III

Seeing the Big Picture

The Plan: A Sample Year in the Life of Your Dog

This chapter lays out a succinct, easy-to-use plan for action that, if followed, will result in a happier, healthier, longer-living pet. Basically a summation of the information already presented, this quick-reference guide will let you know just what to do and when to do it. Broken down into daily, weekly, and monthly, biannual, and annual checklists, you will be able to, at a glance, know what actions on your part will be needed to best insure the extension of your dog's life. Included are recommended nutritional and herbal supplementations and dosages, according to weight. Also included is a section specifying what supplements might help improve digestion and overall metabolism and health in the aging dog, as well as a short section on experimental therapies that are proving to be effective in extending the lives of humans and animals.

Once Every Day

- Feed your dog quality food each day, as defined in Step 5, pp. 100–126. Whatever type of food you decide to feed, it should be nutritious, meat-based, whole-grain, free of unwanted preservatives or chemicals, and rich in the vitamins, minerals, and enzymes necessary for a healthy metabolism. For puppies up to 20 weeks, feed 3 times per day. For puppies between 20 weeks and adulthood, feed 2 times per day. For dogs over this age, feed either 1 to 2 times each day, depending on your schedule and your dog's preferences. Just make sure not to overfeed and risk obesity. For details on feeding, see Step 5, pp. 100–126.

- Give your dog a nutritional supplement each day that includes the following:

Vitamin A (in the form of Beta-carotene)	1500 IU for each 20 pounds of body weight.
Vitamin B-complex:	Follow dosage recommended on the bottle of a brand made especially for pets.
Vitamin C:	500 mg for each 20 pounds of body weight.
Vitamin E:	100 IU daily for each 20 pounds of body weight.
Minerals:	A 20-pound dog should be given 1/5 of the adult human dosage.
Selenium:	Important for the immune system, give 30 mcg daily for each 20 pounds of body weight.
Zinc:	Essential for repair and immune function, a 20-pound dog should be given 5 mg daily.
Glutathione:	A powerful antioxidant, glutathione helps neutralize free radicals. A 20-pound dog should be given 1/5 the adult human dosage.
Lecithin:	Helpful in promoting mental alertness, a 20-pound dog should be given 1/5 the adult human dosage of lecithin oil.

Carnitine:

Known as a "lipotropic" agent (important in helping the liver metabolize toxins), a 20-pound dog should be given 1/5 the adult human dosage.

Choline:

Another lipotropic agent, a 20-pound dog should be given 1/5 the adult human dosage.

Proteolytic enzyme:

Helpful in bolstering your dog's digestive enzyme function, a 20-pound dog should be given 1/5 the adult human dosage.

Herbs:

Available at grocery or health-food stores, you can use these at any time to aid in digestion and regeneration of tissues. For each 20-pounds of weight give 1/5 of the recommended human dosage.

The following herbs can be added frequently to your dog's diet.

Alfafa sprouts
Aloe vera
Astragalus
Basil
Blue-green algae
Burdock root
Cranberry
Dandelion
Echinacea (should be used continuously for no more than 2 weeks)
Garlic (no more than a quarter clove per 20 pounds of dog)
Ginkgo leaf (or gingko biloba)
Ginseng
Grapeseed skin
Goldenseal

Horsetail
Kelp powder
Milk thistle seed
Parsley
Spirulina
Shiitake mushrooms
Thyme
Tumeric (curcuma longa)
Wheat grass

All amounts apply to puppies as well, provided you stick to the weight guidelines. For instance, if an adult dog weighing 20 pounds requires 500 mg of vitamin C per day, a 4-month-old puppy weighing 10 pounds should be given 250 mg.

- Give your dog 2 to 3 tablespoons of plain lactobacillus acidophilus yogurt or lactobacillus capsules each day, to help maintain "good" probiotic bacteria levels in the large intestine.
- Visually check dog's stool for any abnormalities, including blood, undigested food, color change, parasites, or mucous. Also try to observe the color of your dog's urine, which should be a pale yellow, and not clear or dark yellow, red, or brown.
- Observe your dog's elimination habits, to determine whether or not problems such as diarrhea, constipation, or incontinence exist. Notice frequency of bowel movement and urination, and alert your vet if dramatic changes occur.
- Apply commercial tooth gel or colloidal silver to your dog's teeth, using a cotton swab or your clean finger.
- Exercise your dog at least 1 time daily. A 15-minute walk or jog, a romp in a field, or a session with a Frisbee or tennis ball will do.
- Socialize your dog. Try to introduce him to new persons and animals, and take him into reasonably busy areas (on-leash, of course).

- Work on some type of obedience-training exercise for at least 10 minutes, be it sitting, coming, retrieving, or whatever else you desire.
- Observe overall behavior for any abnormalities that might point to illness.

Once Every Week

- Perform a thorough home exam on your dog (see Step 1, pp. 39–58, for details).
- Check his vital signs and weigh him.
- Record your dog's overall weekly condition in a small log book, which can be shown to the vet during checkups, or during time of illness.
- Brush your dog's coat thoroughly and clean his ears.
- Thoroughly clean and disinfect your dog's food and water bowls.
- Take your dog for a 1-hour walk, or take him to a fenced-in off-leash park and let him run.
- Thoroughly clean your yard of fecal matter.

Once Every Month

- Bathe your dog, using a vet-approved shampoo and conditioner. Use a vet-approved herbal flea-and-tick shampoo if necessary. Make sure to brush your dog before bathing.
- Put your adult dog on a 1- or 2-day limited fast feeding him just brown rice or vegetable juice, water, and a vitamin/mineral supplement. During the fast, do not allow the dog to perform strenuous activities such as hiking or prolonged running. Please check with your veterinarian before considering a fast.
- Evaluate your home and dog for any type of parasitic infestations. If found, eliminate them from both as swiftly as possible, then fol-

low up each month with additional treatments. Ask your vet for advice with this. Be particularly aware of fleas and ticks during the warmer summer months. Those in warmer, more humid climates should make sure to give their dogs heartworm pills (per the recommendation of your vet).

- Carefully review the home environment to determine its overall safety (see Step 3, pp. 72–85), particularly if you have a puppy or if you have children in the family. Remember that an adult dog has the reasoning capacity of a two-year-old human child.
- Clean and disinfect the dog's doghouse.
- Teach your dog one new behavior, such as shake, roll over, come, dance, and so forth to keep him mentally stimulated.
- Purchase new food for your dog, if you are feeding a commercial brand. Do not keep dry food around for more than 4 weeks, as it can spoil, or at the very least lose nutritional value. If using canned food, make sure to check expiration dates. Those of you who are homecooking for your pet will of course be buying food more often than this.

Once Every Six Months

- Take any dog over the age of 6–8 years in for a complete checkup with the vet. In addition to having a thorough physical exam performed, request that your pet's stool and urine are analyzed. Also, ask the vet if he or she thinks a blood workup is a good idea.
- Purchase a new safe toy for your dog. Avoid rawhides and real bones, as they can damage or kill your dog. Opt instead for balls, squeeze toys, hard rubber or plastic chew toys, a Frisbee, or some other safe, interesting object that will help your dog pass the time. Make sure the toy is too large to be swallowed, and too tough to be ripped up and eaten piecemeal—and make sure it doesn't contain a component, such as a bell or whistle, that could be accidentally swallowed.

- Check the fencing (or other type of containment device) around your home and yard for gaps or holes, and check your property for any signs of wild animals, such as raccoons, rodents, skunks, and the like. Droppings, burrows, chewed areas, or nests, if found, mean that you have wild animals frequenting your property. If not dealt with, your dog could come into contact with them and be injured, or contract any number of diseases.
- Have your 6-month-old dog castrated or spayed, unless you plan on breeding him or her.

Once Per Year

- Take your dog in for an annual health evaluation and physical exam by your vet. Make sure to take in a stool and urine sample for analysis. The vet should analyze your dog's stool and urine, give her a complete physical, and discuss the option of doing a complete blood workup, to get a clear picture of the state of your pet's health. Also, have your vet do an antibody/titer evaluation each year, which will determine your dog's level of immunity to a variety of diseases, and whether she needs to be vaccinated again.
- Update any needed vaccinations, as per your vet's recommendations. Distemper, parvovirus, hepatitis, and leptospirosis booster shots may need to be given. (The need for vaccinating against hepatitis and leptospirosis is currently under question.) In addition, rabies boosters should be given at 1 year of age and then every 3 years for an adult dog. If your dog is kenneled with other pets on a regular basis, the kennel may require an annual kennel cough booster, which will help prevent this nonfatal but debilitating and highly contagious respiratory illness.
- Have your dog's teeth professionally examined, cleaned, and polished by your vet.
- Reevaluate your dog's diet and his caloric intake, to determine if any changes need to be made. For example, if the dog begins

gaining weight, you may need to either reduce the amount of food served, or switch to a less-caloric diet. Also, a dog could develop a food allergy to something he previously tolerated. If this occurs, you'll need to find a replacement food. Of course, consult your vet before making any significant diet changes, or if you suspect that a food allergy is present.

Supplemental and Behavioral Tips for the Aging Dog

As your dog ages, his digestive tract becomes less efficient at breaking down and absorbing food, due to increased permeability of the intestinal wall (leaky gut syndrome), a decrease in stomach-acid production, as well as a decrease in various digestive enzymes. Also, due to degeneration of muscles, ligaments, tendons, connective tissues, and bones, your older dog is more likely to injure himself, and will take longer to regenerate damaged tissues. To reduce the risk of injury and to improve your older dog's ability to properly digest food, you should:

- Reduce the amount of strenuous activity that the dog participates in, while still maintaining a relatively high level of less-injurious activity, such as walking. Do not allow the older dog to jump down from high places, particularly onto hard surfaces.
- Continue to administer the vitamin/mineral supplements and the lactobacillus acidophilus yogurt or a lactobacillus capsule. Consider consulting your vet regarding possible increases in certain dosages for your aging dog, particularly with the antioxidant nutrients, as these will help bolster the older dog's slowing immune response.
- Carefully monitor your aging dog's weight. If you begin to notice slow but steady weight gain, feed less, or consider switching over to a less-caloric food. Consult your vet before doing so.

- Supplement the older dog's diet with 1 raw egg yolk and one cooked egg white each day, which will provide phospholipids that help protect the aging dog's liver from cumulative affects of organic toxins.
- Sprinkle a small amount of turmeric on the older dog's food 1 time per day, to increase bile production, encourage bowel movement, and remove toxins. Feeding chopped dandelion greens or artichoke leaves will have the same effect.
- Stimulate the older dog's liver and detoxification process by feeding small amounts of cabbage, cauliflower, brussels sprouts, or broccoli. Cook these by steaming or boiling gently, or pulverize and feed raw.
- Help keep the inflammatory response in check by giving the older dog a few ounces of flaxseed, fish, evening primrose, or linseed oil, each day.
- Help strengthen the older dog's sphincter muscles while also promoting mental alertness by supplementing with lecithin oil. Give a 20-pound dog 1/5 of a typical human dosage.
- Treat or prevent constipation and remove toxins by giving the older dog Metamucil. Give a 20-pound dog 1/5 of the normal human dosage.
- Give the older dog suffering from stomach ulcers several ounces of raw cabbage juice each day.
- Give the older dog with decreased stomach-acid production herbal bitters, to help encourage hydrochloric-acid (HC1) output. Give a 20-pound dog 1/5 of the human dosage. Herbal bitters are available in health-food stores.
- Only with approval of your vet, give the older dog with a severe reduction in stomach-acid production supplements of HC1 (hydrocloric-acid tablets). The dosage should be determined by your vet.
- Only with the approval of your vet, give the older dog with a severe reduction in pancreatic enzyme production, enzyme supplementation. The dosage should be determined by your vet.

Experimental Therapies

Current research reveals a number of new strategies that may prove effective in increasing cell regeneration. One behavioral adaptation being studied is caloric restriction, which is theorized to lower overall energy metabolism and slow down the formation of free radicals and their oxidative damage. Tests on mice and monkeys support the idea that a 30 percent reduction in caloric intake seems to increase life span by approximately 25 percent. For the average dog owner, this may mean that decreasing your pet's overall caloric intake slightly may help extend life. Check with your vet before beginning a program of caloric reduction.

Numerous nutritional supplements are now being evaluated to determine whether or not they have true-life extending properties. These include:

LYCOPENE

Classed as a carotenoid (as is beta-carotene), lycopene seems to have great antioxidant properties which can help minimize the formation of free radicals.

ALPHA-LIPOIC ACID

This nutrient seems to enhance the function of other antioxidants, and may help prevent the damage caused by diabetes. It also helps prevent free-radical damage to the DNA within the mitochondria.

ACETYL-L-carnitine (ALC)

Age seems to result in a decrease in the body's production of this nutrient, believed to improve the function of mitochondria (the cell's energy producers). Supplementation may help extend life.

COENZYME-Q-10

Important to mitochondria function, CO Q-10 is a vitaminlike, naturally occurring substance that may also increase the levels of other antioxidants in the body. Numerous studies provide evidence that CO Q-10 is effective in treating heart disease and periodontal disease; it is also thought to have anticancer properties.

PROCYSTEINE

A type of amino acid, procysteine helps increase levels of liver glutathione, an important antioxidant which combats pollutants and toxins in the bloodstream and stops them from damaging the body. It is considered effective in slowing the aging process.

MELATONIN

A naturally occurring antioxidant hormone, melatonin also seems to have a beneficial effect on regulating the body's biological "aging clock" and retarding degeneration of the nervous system.

DHEA

A steroid hormone and antioxidant, DHEA is thought to improve immune function and help prevent cancer. It has been used to treat diabetes, autoimmune diseases, cardiovascular disease, and obesity. Research suggests that supplementation with DHEA is indicated as a means of life extension.

MEGADOSES OF VITAMINS AND MINERALS

Much research is now being done to determine whether high doses of essential vitamins and minerals might profoundly benefit the health and longevity of humans and animals. As many of these nutrients have proven antioxidant qualities, some experts believe that increasing dosages far above minimum daily requirements may help treat disease and extend life. (*Note: Do not attempt to give your dog mega-doses of any nutrient before first discussing it with your vet!*)

L-DEPRENYL

L-Deprenyl is a fascinating antioxidant drug that has recently been licensed to treat Cushing disease in dogs but also has distinct anti-aging properties. Deprenyl therapy can increase the production of the powerful antitoxidant enzymes superoxide dismuatase (SOD) and catalase (CAT). A study using elderly dogs showed that those treated with deprenyl had a significantly greater antibody response. Deprenyl has also been shown to enhance the cognitive functions of geriatric dogs.

LIQUID THYMUS

Liquid thymus extracts have been shown to greatly enhance cellular immunity without displaying toxicity or negative side effects. Because decreased cellular immunity is directly associated with increased aging, liquid thymus therapy should be valuable in an anti-aging program.

GLYCONUTRIENT THERAPY

Research indicates that very specific types of complex plant carbohydrates can produce an impressive increase in immune protection. One of these glyconutrients, acemanin, has been proven to increase immune cell communication and consequently strengthen the immune system.

GENE THERAPY

The correction of a disease by manipulating and transfering genetic material defines the basic goal of gene therapy. In small clinical trials, gene therapy has been successul in treating a very limited number of diseases.

Therapies for Common
Age-Related Disorders

This chapter addresses some of the most common age-related illnesses that, if present in your dog, accelerate the aging process and contribute to overall failing health. Each illness includes a brief explanation of the disorder, diagnostic information, and therapies that may have the best chance of preventing or treating each condition. Meant only as a quick reference guide, owners who suspect the onset of any of these disorders should take their dogs to the vet as soon as possible for accurate diagnosis and treatment. The therapy provided for each disorder should only be administrated after veterinary approval and dosage recommendations.

Arthritis

DESCRIPTION

Characterized by pain and stiffness, arthritis may involve one joint or many and may vary in its severity. In *osteoarthritis*, degeneration of the cartilage in the joint occurs, causing restricted movement and pain. In *rheumatoid arthritis*, an autoimmune disorder actually causes the dog's own body to attack the joints and surrounding soft tissue.

Diagnosis

Usually seen in older dogs, arthritis can often be diagnosed when your vet observes his symptoms including a stiff, painful gait, difficulty rising, or pain and sensitivity to joint manipulation. Your vet may extract fluid from the joint for examination. X rays also may help confirm suspicions and determine the extent of the damage. Blood tests can help diagnose rheumatoid arthritis which has symptoms similar to osteoarthritis, but with more inflammation.

Therapy

- Follow enlightened breeding practices to help reduce the genetic predisposition to problems such as hip dysplasia, kneecap dislocation, and elbow dysplasia (primarily found in large breeds).
- Feed a high-quality meat-based diet, containing whole-grain cereals and avoid chemical additives and food protein that are likely to be allergens.
- Supplement with digestive enzymes, fatty acids, probiotics, and a comprehensive megavitamin and mineral supplement.
- Avoid obesity.
- Observe an enlightened approach to exercise—not too much or too little.
- Observe careful use of antibiotics and anti-inflammatory drugs— avoid if possible.
- Provide adequate rest and physical therapy.
- Identify and eliminate as many allergic substances as possible from the dog's world.
- Improve immune health through diet, stress reduction, and antioxidant therapy.
- Supplement with antioxidant enzymes, vitamins, and minerals (particularly 500 to 1000 mg of vitamin C each day for a medium-sized dog [40 pounds], vitamin E, selenium, and superoxide dismutase and catalase).

- Add vegetables and fiber to the diet, and supplement daily with garlic.
- Consider seeing a veterinary acupuncturist.
- Investigate glucosamine and chondroitin sulfates and other glycoaminoglycan (GAG) therapy. Injections of GAGs in conjunction with injections of antioxidant enzymes and injections of vitamin E and selenium can prove very helpful. If arthritis becomes so severe that it is unresponsive to these therapies, the surgical replacement of the entire joint may be in order.

Bacterial Pneumonia

DESCRIPTION

A bacterial infection of the lungs, pneumonia often preys on older dogs who are susceptible due to their decline in respiratory immune defenses. When harmful bacteria get into the lungs of an older dog with a compromised immune system, they proliferate due to warm, humid, blood-rich conditions.

DIAGNOSIS

The most common signs of bacterial pneumonia are persistent cough and fever, loss of appetite, fatigue, and difficulty breathing, sometimes accompanied by discharge from the nose. X rays, blood tests, and tracheal washes accompanied by a culture often are performed to confirm the diagnosis.

THERAPY

- After confirming the diagnosis, the vet administers the antibiotic best suited to kill the bacteria. This course of medication is followed until the offending contagions no longer infect the lungs. A vet-approved cough medicine also may be administered. Rest and warmth are vital to a dog recovering from pneumonia. A high-quality diet containing all the essential nutrients, accompanied by a daily vitamin/mineral supplement, help your dog's immune system fight the infection from within.

• In place of pharmaceutical antibiotics, the holistic practitioner may recommend herbal "antibiotics" such as garlic, goldenseal, and echinacea. If antibiotics are used for more than a few days, supplementing your dog's food with probiotics (lactobacillus acidophilus) is necessary, as these "good" bacteria are killed off along with the bad. Some vets also use acupuncture to quiet a persistent cough and stimulate the immune system.

Cancer

DESCRIPTION

Cancer is defined as any of a group of diseases that invoke the unchecked growth of cells in one or more organs of the body. Malignant tumors can grow in almost any part of the dog's body, occurring when a cancer-inducing substance (a carcinogen) causes certain genes that control cell growth (called oncogenes) to go haywire. Though hereditary factors play a role in the incidence of many cancers in dogs, the environment also plays a large role. Toxins, pollutants, preservatives, and food additives have all been implicated in playing a role in cancer in dogs. Nutritional deficiencies reduce the immune system's strength, predisposing it to cancer.

DIAGNOSIS

Your vet may diagnose the presence of cancer through the use of blood, urine, or fecal tests, biopsy of suspected tissue, X rays, ultrasound, and physical examination.

THERAPY

Cancer in dogs may be curable or can be put into remission if caught early, depending on the type of cancer.

- Combinations of drug therapy, surgery, and radiation treatments can remove cancer cells, though side effects can be unpleasant or even life-threatening, especially with an older or weaker dog.
- Consider nutritional, herbal, antioxidant, and phytochemical therapies to either replace or complement the more conventional approaches.
- Feed your dog an organic, meat-based, chemical-free, whole-grain diet to build a strong immune system and reduce food toxins—both of which reduce the chances of cancer developing.
- Further eliminate toxins in the dog's air, food, and water to try to prevent the occurrence of cancer.
- Provide fresh cruciferous vegetables, including broccoli, cabbage, cauliflower, and brussels sprouts, and orange fruits and vegetables as well.
- Give your pet megadoses of B-vitamins and mineral supplements that contain up to seventy-four trace minerals.
- Use bottled or filtered water to reduce toxin ingestion.
- Fight free-radical formation by supplementing your dog's diet with proper quantities of antioxidants, enzymes, vitamin and minerals, particularly megadoses of vitamins C and E, carotenoids (e.g., beta-carotene), flavonoids (from fruits, e.g., bioflavonoids), and garlic. Injections of antioxidant enzymes are much more effective than oral supplementation in reducing the free-radical load.
- Ensure that your dog gets enough exercise and rest.
- Reduce stress in your pet's life.
- Neuter your dog by the time he reaches 8 to 10 months of age.
- Avoid obesity.

- Use acupuncture to help maintain a strong, responsive immune system.

Chronic Bronchial Disease (CBD or COPD)

DESCRIPTION

Chronic bronchial disease (or chronic obstructive pulmonary disease [COPD]), a progressive inflammatory disease of the *bronchi* (the airways leading to the lungs), frequently results from unknown causes. Bronchial attacks are more common in the winter, particularly among older dogs. Symptoms include a persistent cough accompanied by abnormal inspiratory and expiratory breathing sounds.

DIAGNOSIS

Your vet is able to properly diagnose the presence of chronic bronchial disease by observation, listening to your dog's breathing, and testing any sputum that might appear. Chest X rays, electrocardiograms, bacterial and fungal cultures, and a heartworm testing may be performed to distinguish CBD from other conditions that have similar symptoms, including heartworm disease, tracheal collapse, bacterial bronchitis, allergic bronchitis, parasitic bronchitis, tumors, and congestive heart failure.

THERAPY

- Ensure that your pet is kept in an environment free of airborne pollutants.
- Humidify his living space by the use of a vaporizer or humidifier.
- Make sure the dog is kept warm and ensure that he gets plenty of rest and minimal exercise and stress, which can aggravate the respiratory tract and stimulate a cough response.

- Use a vet-prescribed bronchial-dilating drug or herbal formula to reduce the cough and make breathing easier.
- Maintain the best nutritive state possible by feeding a high-quality, meat-based, allergen-free diet.
- Give the dog megadoses of vitamins A, C, and E, anti-inflammatory fatty acids, and digestive enzymes containing high levels of lipase.
- Administer (with vet's approval) small amounts of herbal, antibacterial cough medicine when necessary (available at most good health-food stores).
- See a veterinary acupuncturist, who can reduce coughing and dilate the bronchi.

Chronic Ear Inflammation

DESCRIPTION

This type of infection may appear in two forms: recurrent, which can be cleared up and then reappears; or antibiotic-resistant, which never seems to clear up. The cause may be due to bacteria, yeast, or allergens. Although the infections may be the primary problem, often they are secondary, resulting from an allergy or immune-system suppression. Chronic ear infections are very uncomfortable and stressful, and consequently greatly reduce quality of life. Because of the chronic stress these ear infections produce, they very likely weaken the immune system and predispose the animal to other diseases.

DIAGNOSIS

Ear infections can be caused by mites, molds, bacteria, allergens, or foreign bodies in the ear. Laboratory methods include ear cytology (to distinguish between bacteria, yeast, and mites) and checking bacterial cultures and antibiotic sensitivities (to help determine the type of bacteria and what antibiotic is the most effective treatment).

If allergies are suspected as a primary cause, determining the cause of the allergy is crucial to treating the disease.

THERAPY

Check with your veterinarian before trying any of these therapies.

Conventional treatment approaches are:
- Professionally clean and flush the ears of debris and wax, which may require administering an anesthetic to perform a thorough job.
- Apply the appropriate antibiotic, dispensed by your veterinarian.
- Clean the ears daily before applying the antibiotic.
- If the ear is raw or abraded, consider administrating oral antibiotics.
- If the ear is extremely inflamed and scratching is intense, consider an injection of dexamethasone, followed by no more than a few days of cortisone until the inflammation is reduced and the dog is no longer in agony. A protective Elizabethan collar may be necessary to prevent self-mutilation by your dog.

Alternative approaches are:
- Feed a high-quality, meat-based, whole-grain, chemical-free diet. If allergies have been determined as a primary cause, eliminate the allergens from the diet. Give concentrated proteolytic digestive enzymes with meals to attempt to completely remove broken-down grain protein from the intestines, since grains are a common allergen.
- Clean your dog's ears thoroughly with almond or olive oil. If his ears are extremely inflamed and impacted, doing a good cleaning job may require an anesthetic (administered by your vet).
- Infuse the ears with colloidal silver. DMSO is often helpful to transport these therapeutic substances deeper into the tissue surrounding the ear canal.

- Administer vitamins A, C, E, selenium, and zinc, as they are important antioxidants, anti-inflammatories, and immune-system stimulants.
- Administer flaxseed, evening primrose, or fish oils, as they are important sources of natural anti-inflammatories.
- Administer immune stimulants, such as echinacea and garlic, to help knock out the infection.
- See a veterinary acupuncturist to reduce inflammation and treat an underlying allergy.

Chronic Pancreatitis

DESCRIPTION

A serious disorder, involving the inflammation of the pancreas, this condition occurs more often in middle-aged, overweight dogs. It can have major consequences on the health of a dog, even shortening his life span considerably if not properly handled. Caused by infection, injury, autoimmune disease, or in rare cases by an adverse reaction to immune-suppressive drugs, pancreatitis can be painful and recurring. A pancreas afflicted with chronic pancreatitis may lose its ability to efficiently produce pancreatic enzymes, causing maldigestion and malabsorption of nutrients. In addition, the production of insulin and glucagon, hormones necessary for the metabolization of glucose, are severely curtailed, which brings on diabetes, another serious disorder that can considerably shorten the dog's life (discussed later in this chapter).

DIAGNOSIS

Your vet diagnoses pancreatitis in your dog through physical examination, taking a medical history, X rays, blood tests, and fecal tests, which measure enzyme and hormonal outputs of the pancreas.

Diabeteslike symptoms such as excessive thirst or urination, weight loss, or fatigue are all possible.

THERAPY

- Minor bouts of pancreatitis normally are not treated directly. Instead, the condition causing the problem is dealt with, be it infection or injury.
- Fasting may be necessary for a few days to decrease pancreatic activity, while fluid therapy is administered if vomiting and/or dehydration occurs.
- Surgery is rarely called for, though it may be necessary if a tumor is present.
- Digestive-enzyme and hormone-replacement therapies may be necessary if pancreatic degeneration has reached a point where the pancreas is no longer able to produce these in the proper amounts for metabolism to occur.
- Feed a balanced, nutritious, low-fat diet that is free of toxins, which help prevent recurring episodes of pancreatitis in your dog.
- Ensure that whole grains rather than refined sugars are contained in the pet's food.
- Provide digestive enzymes and antioxidants.
- Injections of antioxidant enzymes are preferable to oral supplementation.

Chronic Renal Failure (CRF)

DESCRIPTION

A common cause of death in older dogs, chronic and renal failure is a progressive, degenerative disease that slowly impedes the kidneys' abilities to rid the body of waste products and inhibits its ability to maintain the proper water, acid base, and electrolyte balance.

The kidneys of older dogs become smaller and lighter (compared to those of younger dogs), which directly affects their ability to function. Causes of chronic renal failure are still being explored.

DIAGNOSIS

Frequent urination or incontinence are early signs of renal failure, resulting from increased dilute urine production putting great strain on the bladder and its sphincter. Increased thirst and dehydration (from excess urine production) also appear. Due to progressive dehydration, the kidneys become less able to rid the dog's body of waste, causing a toxic condition called *uremia*. The combination of dehydration and toxin buildup causes fatigue and overall poor health. As toxins build up, the dog becomes sicker and may begin to vomit.

Your vet, when suspecting CRF, performs a standard urinalysis, which identifies dilute urine with high levels of protein. Blood tests may show elevated levels of urea, creatinine, and phosphorus, as well as increased acidity. Catch CRF as early as possible via a blood test and urinalysis; early identification is crucial to treatment.

THERAPY

- Use fluid therapy to reestablish the water, electrolyte, and acid-base balance.
- Change to a higher-quality, lower-protein diet.
- Use antacids to lower the dog's blood phosphorus levels.
- Administer drug therapy to deal with possible anemia.
- Supplement the diet with vitamins, minerals, and antioxidants to reduce free-radical production in the kidneys. Vitamin B_{12} injections are particularly good for treating associated anemia, poor appetite, and weight loss.
- Consider acupuncture, herbal supplements, and homeopathy to encourage kidney function.
- Reduce toxins in your dog's environment.

Chronic Valvular Disease (CVD)

DESCRIPTION

The most common cardiovascular disease in dogs, chronic valvular disease results from the thickening of the mitral and tricuspid heart valves. These valves slowly lose their ability to close properly, allowing blood to leak backward from where it came. This may cause a heart murmur and eventually result in a buildup of fluid in the lungs or abdomen, elevated blood pressure, and an enlarged heart—a condition known as congestive heart failure.

DIAGNOSIS

Coughing, breathing difficulties, weakness, fatigue, fainting, loss of appetite, loss of weight, abdominal distention, and heart murmur are all signs that point to chronic valvular disease. To confirm the diagnosis, your vet listens to your dog's heart and uses X rays, electrocardiograms, and perhaps ultrasound imaging.

THERAPY

- Dogs with a slight heart murmur may not require therapy.
- Those with other signs of CVD, however, may need to be fed a low-sodium diet.
- Diuretics may become necessary.
- In advanced stages, the dog may need additional drug therapy, including the administration of enalapril, digitalis, or nitroglycerine tablets.

Alternative therapies that may prove useful and less toxic in slowing down the degenerative process include:

- Acupuncture.
- Antioxidant supplementation to slow down free-radical damage of the heart cells, especially Vitamin C, E, selenium, and coenzyme Q-10.

- Increased amounts of vitamin/mineral supplementation, including specifically niacin, pyridoxine, zinc, and chromium.
- Herbal supplementation with the dandelion root and hawthorn berry to decrease fluid in the lungs, strengthen the heart, and enhance the immune system. Garlic and cayenne can be added to the diet.
- Regular but restricted exercise each day.

Cushing's Syndrome

DESCRIPTION

Cushing's syndrome may be caused by an abnormally high output of corticosteroid hormones by the adrenal glands, the overuse of prescription corticosteroid drugs, or a tumor on the pituitary gland. The condition may be extremely serious, aging a dog prematurely and leading to fatigue, irritability, high blood pressure, weakened bones, and diabetes.

DIAGNOSIS

Your vet can diagnose the presence of Cushing's syndrome by measuring the levels of hormones present in your dog's blood and urine. You may first suspect a problem when your dog begins to drink and urinate more; he may develop a distended abdomen and poor coat.

THERAPY

- Avoidance or careful use of corticosteroid drugs can help prevent the appearance of Cushing's in your dog. When a dog undergoing regular treatment with corticosteroids is diagnosed with Cushing's, the slow withdrawal of the drug often reverses the condition.
- If the cause is a tumorous growth on the pituitary, chemotherapy may be the only treatment available, as surgery on this area of the

dog's brain is difficult and rarely practiced. Fortunately, the new drug Anipryl is now available to use in place of the much more toxic chemotherapeutic Lysodren.

- Feed a high-quality meat-based diet that is free of toxins, additives, and other unnecessary ingredients to aid in preventing Cushing's syndrome.
- Add antioxidants and enzymes to the diet to help support the immune system and lower the free-radical load.

Degenerative Lumbosacral Stenosis (DLS)

DESCRIPTION

This chronic degenerative disease results in the narrowing of the bony vertebral canal that houses the spinal cord. This compression of the spinal cord where the lumbar vertebrae joins the pelvis causes a variety of symptoms, including pain, loss of coordination, and fecal or urinary incontinence. DLS affects larger breeds more often than smaller ones.

DIAGNOSIS

Your vet diagnoses this condition through physical examination, X rays, and electromyography, a technique that measures nerve conduction. A myelogram may be performed to pinpoint and visualize the area of compression.

THERAPY

- Anti-inflammatory drug therapy may be used to slow down the process of the disease.
- Surgical decompression of the nervous tissue passing through the canal may also relieve pain and restore function, provided nerve damage has not been too severe.

Other therapies for DLS include:

- Rest.
- Antioxidant and anti-inflammatory fatty-acid therapies.
- Acupuncture.
- Chiropractic.
- DMSO, a tropical anti-inflammatory solution that penetrates the unbroken skin and relieves pain and soreness.
- Herbal supplementation with alfalfa, yucca, and licorice root.

Degenerative Myelopathy (DM)

DESCRIPTION

Degenerative myelopathy is a degenerative disease of the thoracic and lumbar spinal cord, wherein the protective myelin sheath covering the spinal cord begins to break down. More common in larger, older pets, DM manifests itself in a slow progressive dysfunction of the dog's hind limbs. Leg movement can become weak and clumsy while reflexes diminish, which later involves fecal and urinary incontinence. In the final stages, the dog cannot stand up and must be lifted to a standing position and supported under the abdomen in order to eliminate waste.

DIAGNOSIS

Your vet diagnoses the condition through physical observation, X rays, a neurological examine, and manipulation of the affected area. You may first suspect a problem when your dog's gait changes and he starts "knuckling over" as he walks; his gait becomes wobbly and unsure, and he may have trouble rising, sitting, or walking up and down stairs. This condition is often confused with arthritis and disk disease.

THERAPY

Though no cure presently exists, hope exists for control over this life-threatening disorder.

- Anti-inflammatory drugs, as well as administering epsilon-aminocaproic acid (EACA), can help prevent inflammation of the nerve sheath and limit the degeneration of tissue.
- Acupuncture.
- Antioxidant therapy to slow down tissue degeneration.
- Chiropractic adjustments.

Diabetes Mellitus

DESCRIPTION

Diabetes mellitus is a serious condition caused by the cells' inability to metabolize sugar in the blood because of a deficiency of insulin or an inability of the cells to respond to insulin. As a result, the sugar stays in the dog's bloodstream and the levels of sugar will be high in his urine. Possible causes for diabetes include genetic abnormalities, pancreatic dysfunction, disorders of the endocrine system, obesity, and a poor diet that is high in sugar and simple carbohydrates. In advanced stages, the disease can result in coma and death.

DIAGNOSIS

The dog suffering from diabetes drinks and urinates frequently, suffers dehydration, and loses weight. Your vet can diagnose diabetes mellitus in your dog through physical examination, and through blood and urine tests for elevated sugar levels and abnormally high or low blood insulin levels.

The goal in treating diabetes is to bring down elevated blood-sugar levels into a normal range and to correct any dehydration and electrolyte imbalances.

- Subcutaneous injections of insulin are begun and continued on a daily basis, while sugar levels in the blood and urine are monitored.
- Managing the diet of a diabetic dog is an extremely important facet in controlling the problem. All refined sugars and simple carbohydrates must be eliminated and replaced with whole grains and complex carbohydrates.
- Correct obesity.
- Antioxidant therapy (especially vitamins C and E, selenium, garlic and goldenseal).
- Increase amounts of omega-6 fatty acids in the diet.
- Supplement the diet with brewer's yeast.
- Increase fiber intake.
- Herbal supplementation, including garlic, aloe vera, kelp, and cayenne (if your dog can tolerate them).
- Mineral therapy, including zinc, chromium, and vanadium.
- Acupuncture may also be effective in stimulating endocrine and pancreatic function, as well as mediating any pain or discomfort.

Epilepsy

DESCRIPTION

Characterized by a diminished level of consciousness, loss of voluntary muscle control resulting in spasms and convulsions, loss of bladder and bowel control, and excess salivation, epileptic episodes in a dog can last from 30 seconds to over several minutes. Often showing up in geriatric dogs, epilepsy also may appear between the ages of 1 and 3. The seizures involve the entire body and are characterized by rigidity, an arched neck, extended front feet, and clenched teeth. These events may come one at a time, days or months apart, or in clusters. Though the cause is not completely understood, epilepsy may have hereditary or congenital roots.

DIAGNOSIS

Your vet is able to diagnose the condition by witnessing a seizure, which could require kenneling the dog at the clinic for a day or more. Extensive tests involving a thorough physical and neurological exam also are called for, as are a blood-chemistry profile, a cardiac evaluation, urinalysis, fecal analysis, and X rays. Brain tumors, heart disease, hypoglycemia (an abnormal decrease of sugar in the blood), hypocalcemia (a deficiency of calcium in the blood), worms, and poisoning are some of the disorders that must be distinguished from true epilepsy in order to diagnose and treat the condition properly.

THERAPY

- When epileptic seizures occur less often than once a month, vets normally do not treat the condition, as the mood-altering and behavioral side effects of the anticonvulsant medications may be more troublesome than the actual condition.
- If the seizures occur more than once a month or are extremely severe in duration or intensity, the vet prescribes anticonvulsants, which help control the problem, but also cause fatigue, excess water consumption, frequent urination, and possible liver damage.
- Acupuncture techniques have been shown to be very helpful in modulating epileptic seizures. In particular, an experimental technique known as "gold-bead embedding" involves the implantation of small gold beads under the skin of the ear and skull at specific acupuncture points. These beads provide continuous

stimulation of the appropriate acupuncture points, which appears to significantly reduce seizure frequency and duration, as well as reducing the dosage levels of the anticonvulsants, when required.

Other therapies that may help include:

- High dosages of vitamins C, B-complex, lecithin, and antioxidants, such as vitamins A, C, and E.
- Elimination of toxins and allergens from the dog's diet, water, and environment.
- Increased amounts of fresh, highly nutritious, meat-based, nontoxic, chemical-free, high-fiber food.
- A 2-day fast once every month.
- Regular, moderate exercise.
- Minimized stress.

Inflammatory Bowel Disease (IBD)

DESCRIPTION

Inflammatory bowel disease is often cyclical, with an inflammation of the intestinal lining that causes repetitive vomiting and/or mucousy diarrhea. The condition often occurs from weekly to monthly intervals, for no apparent reason. It can also be associated with a food allergy.

DIAGNOSIS

Your vet will rule out intestinal parasites and infections through a fecal exam and fecal culture. Physical exams and X rays reveal very little. History taking may reveal a cyclical vomiting and/or mucousy diarrhea. A definitive diagnosis can be reached by taking full thickness biopsies of the intestinal wall, or an endoscopic exploration of the intestinal lining in which tissue samples of the intestinal mucosa and submucosa are taken and then sent to the laboratory for histopathology. An alternative to biopsy and histopathology is to first use anti-inflammatory medication to see if the symptoms of IBD subside.

THERAPY

Conventional approaches are:
- Eliminate the allergic ingredient from the diet.
- Use metronidazole, asulfadiene, or prednisone to reduce inflammation when symptoms flare up.
- Use antispasmodic medication and intestinal protectants.

Alternative approaches are:
- Fast for 2 to 3 days.
- Provide a high-quality, meat-based, whole-grain, chemically free diet that is free of the allergenic ingredient that may have been established through blood testing or an elimination diet. Also add raw or barely cooked meat and steamed vegetables to the diet.
- Fiber supplementation is very important.
- Reduce inflammation and free radicals by supplementing with beta-carotene, vitamins C and E, selenium, sulfur, and flaxseed oil.
- Heal the gut using fructooligosaccharides, probiotics, digestive enzymes, fermentable fiber, and glycoaminoglycans.
- See a veterinary acupuncturist.
- Administer the phytochemical quercetin (found in garlic) and the herb licorice root.

Megaesophagus

DESCRIPTION

Neuromuscular megaesophagus is a chronic disease characterized by a loss of nerve function to the esophageal muscles. The condition causes the muscles to become weak and flaccid, which in turn allows food to accumulate in the esophagus. The esophagus then becomes distended, often resulting in pneumonia, regurgitation, and malnourishment. The cause of this condition is unknown, though thyroid disorders, poisoning, and immune disorders are all suspects.

DIAGNOSIS

A dog suffering from this condition often regurgitates soon after eating a meal. Accompanying signs include increased appetite, weakness, dehydration, an enlargement of the neck (particularly after eating), belching, and bad breath. Your vet is able to diagnose the condition through physical examination, X rays, endoscopic examination, nerve conduction tests, and in some cases, biopsies of affected tissues.

THERAPY

- Once a diagnosis is made, treatment is normally directed at reestablishing conduction. While that's happening, your vet needs to ensure that your dog receives proper nutrition. This may involve feeding very small amounts of liquid food numerous times each day, while holding the dog's head, neck, and body in an upright, or more vertical position (to take advantage of gravity).
- In serious cases, a feeding tube may be placed surgically into the stomach so that food can bypass the weakened esophagus.
- Some veterinarians have had good results using electroacupuncture to stimulate the affected nerves, thereby restoring muscle action to the esophagus.
- In conjunction with the acupuncture treatments, supplementation with B-complex vitamins and choline also may encourage nerve conduction.

Periodontal Disease

DESCRIPTION

Periodontal disease refers to a degeneration disorder of the tissues surrounding and supporting your dog's teeth. Though not life-threatening in and of itself, severe periodontal disease can result in loss of teeth and can damage the dog's heart, liver, kidneys, and lungs as a result of oral bacteria and bacterial toxins getting into the blood-stream. Food deposits, if not routinely removed from your dog's teeth, begin to form plaque, ultimately leading to bacterial infection, inflammation, and disease of the gums. As the gums recede, they open up a pathway for more bacteria, which eventually undermines the anchoring of the teeth and causes tooth loss.

DIAGNOSIS

Tartar and plaque buildup is evidenced by the formation of brown stains on the teeth, particularly the molars and premolars; swollen, tender, or receding gums; bad breath, bleeding gums, and loose or missing teeth. Your vet can quickly determine if periodontal disease is present through direct examination of each tooth and the surrounding gum.

THERAPY

Prevention, through limiting the formation of bacteria in your dog's mouth, is the key.

- Use a bacteria-reducing gel or paint colloidal silver on the dog's teeth, which does not require brushing.
- Brush your dog's teeth at least once a week, with a vet-approved canine toothpaste and toothbrush. If your pet can handle daily brushing, it is certainly beneficial.

- Use a veterinary-prescribed slow-release medicated patch that adheres to the inside of the cheeks and releases an antibacterial medication. Have your dog's teeth cleaned at least once each year by your vet.
- Supplement his diet with beta-carotene, vitamin C, and coenzyme Q-10.
- If your dog has already lost a lot of teeth to periodontal disease, ensure that you serve his food in pieces soft enough to be swallowed and digested easily. Accomplish this by soaking the food for 10 minutes in warm water or putting it through a food processor. However, continue to brush the dog's remaining teeth, and have your vet perform annual or biannual dental exams and cleanings to prevent further decay.
- Next to superior nutrition, regular home and professional dental hygiene is the most important measure a pet owner can take to prolong his or her dog's life.

Wobbler's

DESCRIPTION

Also known as cervical vertebral instability, wobbler's involves compression of the spinal cord in the necks of larger breeds, especially the Doberman pinscher. This compression results in a slow but sure loss of strength and coordination in all four limbs, particularly in the rear ones, resulting in a wobbly, unsure gait. The cause of this compression can be a narrowing of the vertebral canal, degenerative changes in the vertebral disk cartilage, protrusion of the vertebral disk, an overdevelopment of ligaments, or an instability of the cervical vertebral joints, especially in the area of cervical vertebrae 6 and 7. (If Wobbler's causes a young dog to become severely uncoordinated or endure great pain, it could result in a decision to euthanize.)

DIAGNOSIS

Your vet can diagnose wobbler's through observation of the dog's gait, various types of neurologic testing, and the use of plain X rays and myelograms.

THERAPY

- The standard conventional treatment for this progressive condition is steroid therapy, rest, and neck bracing to immobilize the weakened joint.
- Surgery may be used to decompress the spinal cord and restabilize the effective joint; however, its success rate is not high and a dog could be further impaired postsurgery.

Other therapies include:
- Acupuncture and chiropractic.
- Antioxidant supplementation, especially vitamins C, E, selenium, and sulfur.
- Vitamin and mineral supplementation, especially manganese, selenium, and sulfur.
- Glycoaminoglycan therapy to help strengthen ligaments and other joint-affiliated connective-tissue structures.
- Increasing use of omega-3 and omega-6 fatty acids in the diet.
- Elimination of as many toxins as possible from food, water, and air (use air and water filtration systems if possible).
- Feeding a fresh, nutritionally balanced diet that includes lightly cooked or raw meat with some steamed vegetables and whole grains.

A Time for Letting Go

Extending the lives of our dogs indefinitely would be wonderful, but genetics do not allow that to happen. Your dog's hereditary makeup does have the last word; eventually, your canine friend will develop one or more conditions that either proves fatal or increasingly painful. When a dog's bowel and bladder functions no longer remain under her control, her senses no longer function, her appetite is gone, and arthritis or other joint diseases (i.e., disc protrusion) combine to make simple movement unbearable, you should sit down with your trusted veterinarian and have a frank discussion about your options. A vet who is familiar with your dog and her medical history is able to say whether or not a condition is treatable or irreversible; he will strive to determine if maintaining the animal in a relatively pain-free state is possible. Conditions such as severe arthritis or diabetes may be eased through nutritional and drug therapies, improving the quality of life enough to remove euthanasia from the list of options.

Making these types of medical evaluations is the job of a competent, caring vet; trust him or her to know if a seemingly painful, severe symptom can actually be treated effectively enough to make the geriatric dog's life worth living. Understand that no vet, particularly one who knows you and your dog, wants to arbitrarily and needlessly end the life of a valued pet. If he or she determines, however, that the medical problems are progressive and irreversible, you should listen seriously and give adequate consideration to the advice. A loving owner often prolongs the life of a suffering animal simply to postpone the inevitable, which is unfair and often borders on being cruel.

A dog, if optimally cared for, should enjoy a long, healthy life. Some dogs may live as long as twenty years, though the average is closer to ten to fifteen. We bond as friends and family, share good times and bad, and make each other feel happy and loved. In fact, a dog can often be more forgiving and empathetic than many persons in our lives. No wonder we have such a difficult time deciding what to do when the end is near.

The loss of a dog can be especially painful to a single person, who does not have the added emotional support of many family members. In these cases, a dog becomes friend, child, sibling, confessor, and perhaps a substitute spouse. The death of such an animal can be devastating.

Having a terribly ill dog put to sleep is, in my opinion, a courageous and kind act, provided you have conferred with your vet and family and all agree on this course of action. Have no worry that the process of euthanasia is painful or uncomfortable, as it simply involves the intravenous injection of an overdose of a commonly used anesthetic drug. Death comes almost instantaneously, *without pain.*

A number of dogs do pass away due to natural causes. Older dogs usually die from kidney or heart failure, and younger adults by accidental death. A large number, however, do not go peacefully; a strong heart continues to beat, even though the rest of the body has ceased to function properly, and begins to cause the animal great pain, as in the case of severe arthritis.

The decision to euthanize should be made carefully, and by all family members. (Although small children should be in on the discussion, they should not be involved in the actual decision.) If one family member is vehemently against putting the dog to sleep, consider waiting a few days until that person has had time to reflect on the situation or talk to the vet or a counselor. Also encourage that person to spend some time alone with the dog, which may help him or her to understand and to find the courage to reluctantly agree. If he or she still do not agree, the procedure should be put off temporarily. Remember, however, that waiting too long would be cruel if the animal in question is in pain.

Once the decision to euthanize has been made, ask the vet to explain the procedure to you in detail. Though some vets perform the procedure in your home, most insist on doing it in the clinic both to have access to the facilities, necessary supplies, and personnel and to deal with any complications that may occur, such as an unpredictable reaction to the drug or drugs used. You can and should remain with your pet during the entire procedure, and should have a few minutes afterward to be alone with the departed pet. Your vet does not require you to be present if you do not wish to be. Some owners are not capable of dealing with the emotions; others actually suffer a medical problem, such as hyperventilation or a panic attack, due to the stress of the situation. If you feel the ordeal would be too anguishing, do not force the issue. Consider bringing a friend with you for support and to drive you home, as your emotions could cause you difficulty in operating a vehicle. Do not bring young children or the elderly if they suffer from heart problems.

If your vet is performing the procedure in your home, consider removing all other pets and young children from the area. The death of their beloved friend can be very upsetting, and may promote undesirable behaviors and unnecessary trauma.

DISPOSITION OF THE BODY

Before having your dog euthanized, you need to consider just what to do with the remains. Your veterinarian should explain all the options beforehand, and offer to forward the body to the appropriate facility, such as a crematorium or pet cemetery. Your options include:

Home Internment

Taking the dog home and burying her in the location of your choice, on your property, is an option preferred by many. It may be difficult or impossible for those without property or residents of an urban areas. Many municipalities have laws prohibiting the burial of pets within residential areas, so check with your local humane society, the police, or city hall to find out what is permitted.

Pet Cemeteries

Available in many areas, this option provides your pet with a formal burial, complete with casket, burial plot, gravestone with inscription, and even a service if you desire. Potentially expensive, many owners may not be able to afford this, especially with all the extra charges that can pile up. Some owners, however, need the ritual of an official burial in order to feel they have paid the proper respects and to help them get through the grieving process. Your vet or the Yellow Pages can refer you to a competent pet mortuary.

Cremation

Many communities have pet-cremation facilities available. A less-expensive option to an official burial, your canine friend's ashes can be placed in the container of your choice and kept in your home, if you desire. Your vet or the Yellow Pages can direct you to an appropriate facility. (Note: If you choose this option, ask for a written statement from the facility director that you will be assured of receiving only your loved one's ashes.)

Coping with the Loss

The weeks following the euthanization of your dog are very difficult. You may feel great loss and sorrow and even blame yourself for your pet's death, experiencing feelings of profound guilt in the process. The grieving process is natural and inevitable and must be dealt with in your own way, but resist feeling that you have done something wrong. Take comfort in knowing that you relieved your good friend of terrible pain, which you would not want to endure for very long, if given a choice.

Grieving for a pet can be made less painful in several ways. First, make sure to keep friends and family close by, to help support you during your time of need and loss. Talk about the event and about your departed pet; laugh (and cry) about all the crazy, fun things you did together. Interact with other dogs if possible; your other pets at home can be very comforting to you. Remember to be there for them as well, as they are upset and confused by the loss of a valued pack member.

Consider making a small cash donation to a local animal shelter in your departed pet's name or even planting a tree in her memory. Above all, realize that your dog is no longer suffering needlessly, and that she was fortunate to have a devoted, loving owner and a good life.

Wait at least a few months before considering the adoption of another dog. The grieving process can sometimes make us do impulsive ill-advised things; rushing out the next day and adopting one or two orphaned puppies might sound comforting, but you won't be emotionally ready—or capable of calmly and objectively choosing a new pet. Give your mind and your heart some time to settle down before acquiring a new dog. Waiting for a new pet is also a way of showing the proper amount of respect for your departed friend.

Another option is to get a puppy or adult dog well before the end of your resident dog's life. The benefits of doing so are twofold. First, the new dog can model her behavior after the established, well-behaved pet. Second, when the end does come, your loving canine friend is there to support you and make you laugh during your sadness.

If you find that you are having profound difficulty dealing with the loss of your dog, do not hesitate to see a therapist who specializes in grief counseling. He or she may be a great comfort and might even direct you to a pet-loss support group, which could provide the necessary empathetic atmosphere for helping you make it through the tough times. Others, who find comfort in talking to their pastors or priests, should not hesitate to reach out to these spiritual sources.

Conclusion

This book has provided you with medical, behavioral, and nutritional guidelines that, if followed, improve the health and well-being of almost any dog, whether a mixed-breed survivor or a purebred champion. No matter where a dog comes from or what she looks like, she can live a longer, fuller life, provided you follow the ten guidelines that have been emphasized and reemphasized throughout the book.

1. FEED YOUR DOG THE MOST NUTRITIOUS, WELL-BALANCED DIET POSSIBLE

Though the book endorses a properly formulated, homecooked diet using the freshest ingredients possible, certain commercial foods can provide the essential nutrients, especially when supplemented daily with fresh raw meat, vitamins, minerals, beneficial bacteria, and plant enzymes. The key is making sure that the essential nutrients are present in the food, and that it is free of chemical preservatives, additives, coloring agents, hormones, antibodies, and any other potential toxin. By doing so, you support cell regeneration and overall good health.

2. ELIMINATE AS MANY TOXINS AS POSSIBLE FROM YOUR DOG'S WORLD

The dog's food, air, and water should be as clean and fresh as possible, to avoid overloading the immune and inflammatory systems and forming life-threatening diseases, such as cancer or liver disease. This avoidance is especially important for the aging animal, whose regenerative and immune powers are not quite what they used to be.

3. CREATE THE SAFEST ENVIRONMENT POSSIBLE

Ensuring that toxic materials such as antifreeze, paint thinner, or poisonous plants are kept away from the curious dog does much to preserve good health. Also checking that unsafe conditions such as inadequate confinement, exposed wires, dangerous wild animals, or unsafe traffic conditions are kept away from your pet prevents unfortunate and heartbreaking accidents or escapes from cutting short the life of your happy, vibrant friend. As the older dog is not as agile as she used to be, making her environment as safe and carefree as possible becomes essential.

4. ACQUIRE AND UTILIZE THE SERVICES OF A COMPETENT, CARING VETERINARIAN

As healthy as your dog may appear to be, a qualified vet is able to catch subtle signs of a potentially serious illness long before you are. Yearly exams, blood tests, urinalysis, judicious vaccination, teeth cleanings, and nutritional and behavioral consults with your vet help prevent disease, and keep your pet in peak shape. A good vet is your dog's secret weapon; use him or her whenever you are in doubt and make sure to get that annual health checkup, even if your dog seems fit. As your dog ages, seeing the vet more often helps minimize the effects of time.

5. FIGHT FREE RADICALS

A key to maintaining your dog's cellular health is to fight free-radical formation through the use of antioxidant therapy. This is one of the best ways to substantially lengthen your dog's life, especially in the older dog, whose organ systems need this essential therapy to slow the degenerative process.

6. Support Your Dog's Immune System and Inflammatory Processes

Strengthen your pet's immune system and inflammatory processes by providing all of the essential nutrients (especially vitamins, minerals, fatty acids, and antioxidants) and eliminating toxins from the environment. Supplementing with specific herbs can provide powerful immune stimulation, and can modulate over- or underactive inflammatory processes. This creates a surplus of immune strength, allowing your dog to be adequately prepared to fight any illnesses or infections that might beset her. Ensuring that her immune system stays strong right into old age helps extend her life substantially.

7. Train Your Dog Properly

A poorly behaved dog is in constant danger of hurting herself in some way. By teaching her rules, you create boundaries, build her confidence, and establish the leadership hierarchy she needs to feel safe. A dog without leadership or rules is out of control and insecure, two conditions that can easily lead to injury or illness. No dog is too young or too old to learn, though remember that the older animal takes a bit longer to absorb new information.

8. Ensure that Your Dog Gets Sufficient Rest, Exercise, and Proper Hygiene

Rest is a key ingredient to cellular regeneration. Any dog not getting enough rests suffers inadequate regeneration of organ systems, thereby shortening her life. The older dog needs more rest than the younger animal, as her ability to regenerate tissues slows down with age. Exercise is crucial to health and long life, as it stimulates all of the dog's organ systems, helps build muscle and bone, and strengthens the cardiovascular and repository systems. The older dog should be exercised each day, though not as vigorously as a younger animal. Keeping your pet's eyes, ears, teeth, and coat clean will greatly improve the strength of your pet's immune system.

9. REDUCE STRESS

A nervous, agitated dog is not able to remain healthy, as the stress she suffers constantly overstimulates her immune, regulatory, and inflammatory systems. This overstimulation eventually causes exhaustion, which opens up the pathway for illness and infection. Training, socializing, massaging, and fair and kind treatment all help lower stress and create a well-adjusted dog. Never hit or yell at a dog, as this is unfair, and only increases stress and illness. Reducing stress in an older animal often involves making her environment more comfortable and dealing with health issues quickly and efficiently. For instance, relieving the pain of an arthritic hip helps reduce an older dog's stress, allowing her to live a healthier life.

10. EMBRACE BOTH CONVENTIONAL AND ALTERNATIVE THERAPIES

Turning your nose up on either conventional or alternative therapies for your dog shortchanges her, and perhaps prevents healing from occurring. Conventional drugs, diagnosis, tests, judicious vaccination, and surgical techniques have saved thousands of dogs' lives; to turn your back on these methods is senseless and counterproductive. Likewise, alternative treatments such as herbs, acupuncture, massage, and chiropractic help prevent disease and maintain good health. Utilizing a combination of both therapies can keep your dog healthier and happier.

11. SUPPORT YOUR DOG'S INTERNAL DETOXIFICATION AND DIGESTION PROCESSES

Provide your dog with nutrients, herbs, and supplements that enhance digestion and absorption, strengthen the intestinal mucosal lining, nourish the beneficial intestinal bacteria, support the liver's detoxification mechanism, and encourage toxin elimination from the body. A 1- to 2-day partial fast each month is highly beneficial.

Your dog is your friend, guardian, and family. You love her. No one wants to see her age and become ill before her time. Hopefully, the advice given in this book has enlightened you to a number of techniques to help keep your loving canine friend around much longer, so that you can enjoy the mutual feelings you have for each other—for longer than you ever expected.

Appendix A
Canine First Aid

Emergency Techniques

CARDIOPULMONARY RESUSCITATION (CPR)

CPR, a commonly practiced lifesaving technique for humans, can be performed on dogs as well, though it is rarely needed. The need may arise, however, due to trauma. Signs that CPR is necessary include no pulse or respiration and unconsciousness. Begin CPR as soon as you discover that no respiration or heartbeat can be detected, and continue it until a veterinarian can assist you. Without CPR, the dog may die or suffer permanent brain damage.

If Your Dog Stops Breathing, but Has a Pulse

1. Place him on his side, open his mouth, pull out his tongue, and check for any foreign objects that might be lodged in the back of the mouth.
2. Clear away any mucous or blood, then close the dog's mouth and place your mouth over his muzzle, *completely covering the nose.*
3. Blow easily into the nose and watch for the chest to expand. Repeat 12 times per minute until the dog begins breathing on his own or until you get to your veterinary clinic.

If Your Dog Has No Pulse or Respiration

Under these conditions, CPR needs to be combined with cardiac compressions in order to save the dog's life. Though it helps to have another person there to perform the compressions while you continue artificial respiration, you can do it by yourself.

1. Between each breath (given about every 5 seconds), place the heel of your hand over the dog's heart (at about the fifth rib up,

just behind where the front limb attaches to the body), and press down quickly with moderate pressure, then release. (With a small dog, you may need to use 4 or even 3 fingers instead of the heel of your hand.) The ribs should compress about 1 inch. Compress the chest in this way 5 times between each breath.

2. Continue this procedure until you get to the vet (hopefully someone is driving you there and you are in the backseat of a car) or until the dog is breathing on his own with a normal pulse. Use your best judgment as to how long to continue administering CPR. If the dog does not respond within 15 minutes and there is no chance of getting to a vet, it may be prudent to stop.

THE HEIMLICH MANEUVER

A dog can choke if a large piece of food or a toy gets caught in his throat. If you cannot dislodge the object with your hand, forceps, or tweezers, perform the Heimlich maneuver.

1. With the dog lying on his side, place the heel of your hand just below the last rib (where the diaphragm is) and give 2 or 3 quick inward pushes. This forces air up the windpipe, hopefully dislodging the object.

2. With a larger dog, you may be able to actually get behind the animal and perform the Heimlich maneuver in the same manner used on humans—by wrapping your arms around the pet, placing one fist into his abdominal area just below his sternum and last rib, and then pushing the fist sharply inward, using the other hand as an additional power source.

3. Whether you are immediately successful or not, make every effort to get to an emergency clinic, preferably with your pet and you in the backseat of a car being driven by a friend.

Treating Wounds

SMALL CUTS OR ABRASIONS

Trim away hair with scissors or an electric trimmer, taking care not
to irritate the wound. Flush the wound with 3% hydrogen peroxide
and clean the wound with a disinfectant soap. Flush with hydrogen
peroxide again, then apply an antibiotic powder or ointment. Dress
the wound if possible with a gauze wrapping and adhesive tape.

LARGE WOUNDS

Perform the same procedure as with Small Cuts, then get to the vet
as soon as possible, as the wound may need stitches. If it is bleeding steadily, apply pressure to it with a clean gauze pad or cloth. A
tourniquet should only be used if a wound on a limb is bleeding pro-
fusely. To apply a tourniquet, tightly tie a length of fabric around the
appendage, directly above the wound. To avoid tissue death, you
will need to loosen the tourniquet every five minutes for thirty seconds at a time.

BURNS

Apply cool water or ice to the affected area, cover with an antisep-
tic cream and a clean gauze pad, then seek veterinary help. Burns
can have dire consequences, and should not be taken lightly.

BREAKS AND FRACTURES

After carefully bringing the dog indoors, splint the affected limb
with layers of clean cloth wrapped around a stiff piece of cardboard,
wood, or rolled newspaper and an adhesive tape (masking or duct
tape can also be used) then get to the vet immediately.

CAR ACCIDENTS

If your dog has been hit by a car, realize that he is frightened and may bite defensively. You may want to wrap and tie a cloth strip around his muzzle to prevent biting. Next, carefully move a large blanket underneath the injured animal and then, with the help of a friend, gently lift the blanket and dog into a car. Take him to the nearest emergency clinic as soon as possible. Have one person stay in the backseat with the dog to calm him and if necessary, to control bleeding, by applying pressure.

POISONING

Obtain and keep a sample of the toxic substance, then call your vet. He or she will advise you whether to induce vomiting by using salt water, or syrup of ipecac, or 3% hydrogen peroxide. Or he or she may advise you to force-feed the dog water, milk, or even activated charcoal in order to absorb, dilute, or deactivate the poison. Then get the dog to the vet as soon as possible.

Appendix B
The In-Home Canine Pharmacy

Should an emergency arise, you will have saved time by having a preassembled kit of emergency supplies on hand. Place the following items in a box and keep it in a convenient location.

Activated charcoal
Adhesive tape (1-inch-wide roll)
Antibiotic ointment (such as Neosporin)
Aspirin
Blanket
Cotton gauze pads (3-inch square)
Cotton gauze roll (3-inch wide)
Cotton swabs (cotton-tipped applicators)
Disinfectant soap
Dramamine (for motion sickness)
Hydrogen peroxide (3%)
Kaopectate
Canine ear cleaner
Milk of magnesia
Penlight (small)
Pepto-Bismol
Petroleum jelly
Rectal thermometer
Rubbing alcohol
Scissors and tweezers
Styptic powder or flour
Syrup of ipecac (to induce vomiting)
Wound antibiotic powder or colloidal silver

Appendix C
Toxic Substances

COMMON TOXIC PLANTS

Azalea
Bean plant leaves
Cactus
Crocus
Daffodil
Dieffenbachia
Hemlock
Hydrangea
Ivy
Lily
Marijuana
Mistletoe
Mushroom
Narcissus
Nightshade
Oleander
Philodendron
Poinsettia
Potato leaves
Rhododendron
Tobacco
Tomato leaves
Walnuts
Yews

OTHER TOXIC SUBSTANCES IN THE HOME

Alcohol
Antifreeze

Bleach
Dishwashing liquid
Drain cleaner
Gasoline or motor oil
Paint and paint thinner
Pesticides
Shellac
Solvents
Turpentine
Varnish

Appendix D
Health Maintenance Information

PREVENTIVE HEALTH MAINTENANCE CHECKLIST

Thoughts on what constitutes proper routine vaccination are presently in a state of flux. An increasing number of veterinarians are convinced that we are overvaccinating our pets, and therefore discourage blind routine yearly vaccination. These veterinarians believe that routine yearly boostering is unnecessary for most pets, and that this practice can lead to overstimulation of the immune system, eventual immune system suppression, and in rare instances, tumor formation. Instead of blind routine yearly boostering, a growing number of veterinarians are recommending yearly testing of dogs' blood antibodies level (an antibody titer) against different viral diseases. If the values of blood antibodies are within what is considered to be a protective range, then these pets are vaccinated only once every 3 years, or perhaps even more extended intervals. If the antibody titer is not within a protective range, the dog may be boostered at that time.

Keeping that in mind, here are the traditionally accepted recommendations for routine boostering and other routine preventive health procedures:

Vaccinations:

Rabies	1- or 3-year boostering, depending on the dog's age and on individual state requirements
Distemper/hepatitis/ leptospirosis	yearly boostering
Parvovirus	yearly boostering
Kennel cough	yearly boostering if required for boarding or obedience training
Lyme disease	yearly boostering if your dog frequents tick-infested areas populated by deer

Testing and examinations:

Physical exam	yearly; semiannually for dogs over 8 years of age
Stool exam	2 to 3 times a year
Blood screening	yearly; semiannually for dogs over 8 years of age
Heartworm testing	yearly; semiannually for dogs not on preventive medicine
Urinalysis evaluation	yearly; semiannually for dogs over 8 years of age
Dental exam and routine prophylaxis	1 or 2 times yearly, depending on rapidity of tartar formation
Castration or ovariohysterectomy (spaying)	usually by 8 months of age

QUESTIONS YOU CAN ANSWER IN PREPARATION FOR SEEING YOUR VETERINARIAN

1. What is the major concern that brought you and your pet to the clinic?
2. When did you first notice the problem?
3. What was the first definite sign of illness?
4. List, in order of appearance, any other symptoms you have noticed. Which are still present? Have any improved or worsened?
5. What have you done to treat the problem? And has treatment helped?
6. Have you previously taken your pet to a veterinarian for the same problem? If so, what tests were performed and what treatment administered? What helped? What didn't?
7. How are the dog's appetite, thirst, and elimination habits?
8. Have you noticed any changes in behavior, gait, or breathing?
9. If lameness exists, which leg does the dog favor?

If you have been keeping a medical log on your dog, bring it in to show the vet, as information in it might help with diagnosis.

Normal Vital Signs

A dog's vital signs give you a glimpse into the state of her health. If your dog's vital signs differ substantially from any of the following, see your vet as soon as possible.

Temperature:	100.5° to 101.5° (smaller dogs can have normal temperatures that run up to a degree higher than larger animals).
Resting pulse:	75 to 120 beats per minute (smaller dogs have faster resting heartbeats that can be 10 to 20 percent higher than larger animals).
Respiration:	10 to 30 breaths per minute, depending on the dog's size. A Chihuahua, for example, would be on the high end of the range, whereas a St. Bernard would be near the low end.

About the Authors

JOHN M. SIMON, D.V.M., owns a private practice, Woodside Animal Hospital, in Royal Oak, Michigan. A graduate of the Michigan State University School of Veterinary Medicine, Dr. Simon has more than thirty years of experience in conventional and alternative pet care. In 1982, Dr. Simon became Detroit's first certified veterinary acupuncturist; in 1996, he received his certificate from the American Veterinary Chiropractic Association. Dr. Simon is a past president of the Oakland County Veterinary Medical Association (OCVMA) and has served as both an officer and board member of the Southeastern Michigan Veterinary Medical Association (SEMVMA). In 1993, he began hosting his own weekly cable TV talk show, *Your Pet's Good Health*. Dr. Simon has written several books, including *Basic Bird Care & Preventive Medicine*, *What Your Dog Is Trying to Tell You*, and *What Your Cat Is Trying to Tell You*. He has also written a regular column in Detroit's *Daily Tribune* since 1983, and has contributed extensively to pet-care magazines such as *Natural Pet*. Dr. Simon lives in Franklin Village, Michigan, with his wife and two children.

STEVE DUNO is a freelance writer residing in Seattle, Washington. A native New Yorker, Steve has coauthored four books, including *Choosing a Dog*, *Leader of the Pack*, *Show Biz Tricks for Cats*, and *The Everything Cat Book*. He has also published fiction, and is currently working on a novel, a new pet-care book, and an instructional book on golf. Steve has appeared on television and radio, and has written for *Slate*, an on-line magazine. He lives with his nine-year-old rottweiler mix, Louie.